WoMeN's GLiBBer

State-of-the-Art
Women's Humor

Edited
by
Roz Warren

The Crossing Press, Freedom CA 95019

Library of Congress Cataloging-in-Publication Data

Women's glibber: state-of-the-art women's humor/ edited by Roz Warren.
p. cm.
ISBN 0-89594-549-5
1. American wit and humor—Women authors. 2. Women—Humor. 3. Feminism—
Humor. 4. Women—Caricatures and cartoons.
I. Warren, Rosalind, 1954- .
PN6231.W6W66 1992
810.8'09287—dc 20

92-11276
CIP

"Preacher Don't Send Me" by Maya Angelou from *I Shall Not Be Moved* by Maya Angelou. Copyright © 1990 by Maya Angelou. Reprinted by permission of Random House, Inc. "Are You a Real Jock?" by Alison Bechdel from *Dykes to Watch Out For*. Copyright © Alison Bechdel. Reprinted by permission of Firebrand Books (Ithaca, New York). "You Are What You Eat," "The Referral," and "Naturally Resourceful" by Alison Bechdel from *New, Improved! Dykes to Watch Out For*. Copyright © 1990 Alison Bechdel. Reprinted by permission of Firebrand Books (Ithaca, New York). "Creative Visualization" by Alison Bechdel from *Dykes to Watch Out For: The Sequel*. Copyright © 1992 Alison Bechdel. Reprinted by permission of Firebrand Books (Ithaca, New York). Cartoons by Jennifer Berman are copyright © 1991 Jennifer Berman (P.O. Box 6614, Evanston, IL 60204). Reprinted by permission of the artist. Cartoons by Claire Bretecher from *Frustration* by Claire Bretecher. Copyright © 1982 by Claire Bretecher. Used by permission of Grove Press, Inc. Material by Stephanie Brush. Copyright © 1992 Tribune Media Services Inc. Reprinted by permission. Cartoons by Roz Chast are copyright © Roz Chast and copyright © The New Yorker Magazine, Inc. Reprinted with the permission of Wylie, Aitken & Stone, Inc. and The New Yorker Magazine, Inc. Cartoons by Barbara Brandon from *Where I'm Coming From* by Barbara Brandon. Copyright © Universal Press Syndicate. Reprinted by permission of Universal Press Syndicate. "Conversations with Joann" from *Nobody's Rib* by Nora Dunn. Copyright © 1991 by Nora Dunn. Reprinted by permission of HarperCollins Publishers. "Dear Michael" by Taffy Field from *Short Skirts*. Copyright © 1989 by Taffy Field. Reprinted by permission of Tilbury House Publishers (Gardiner, Maine). "Off Ramp" by Polly Frost. Reprinted by permission. Copyright © Polly Frost. Originally in *The New Yorker*. "Equal Time" and "Codicil" from *Love Trouble is My Business* by Veronica Geng. Copyright © 1988 by Veronica Geng. Reprinted by permission of HarperCollins Publishers. "Housecleaning" by Nikki Giovanni from *Cotton Candy on a Rainy Day*. Copyright (1978) Nikki Giovanni. Reprinted by permission of the author. Cartoon by Cathy Guisewitte copyright © Universal Press Syndicate. Reprinted by permission of Universal Press Syndicate. Material by Molly Ivins from *Molly Ivins Can't Say That, Can She?* by Molly Ivins. Copyright © 1991 by Molly Ivins. Reprinted by permission of Alfred A. Knopf, Inc. "Menu" and "Memo" by June Jordan from *Naming Our Destiny: New and Selected Poems* by June Jordan. Copyright © 1989 by June Jordan. Used by permission of the publisher, Thunder's Mouth Press. Excerpt from *Jewish as a Second Language* by Molly Katz. Copyright © Molly Katz. Reprinted with permission of Workmen Publishing. "Land of Hopefully and Glory" by Florence King. Copyright © 1989 by Florence King from the book *Reflections in a Jaundiced Eye*. Reprinted by permission of St. Martin's Press, Inc. Excerpt from *Allegra Maud Goldman* by Edith Konecky. Copyright © 1976, 1987 by Edith Konecky. Published 1990 by The Feminist Press at CUNY. Reprinted by permission of the publisher. Cartoons by Annie Lawson from *Brilliant Advice!* and *More Brilliant Advice!* Copyright © Annie Lawson. Reprinted by permission of the artist. "Pointers for Pets" from *Social Studies* by Frank Lebowitz. Copyright © 1981 by Fran Lebowitz. Reprinted by permission of Random House, Inc. "My Favorite Vacation" by Penny S. Lorio. Copyright © 1991 Penny S. Lorio. Reprinted by permission of the author. Cartoons by K. LeMieux "Lyttle Women" copyright © 1992 by King Features Syndicate, Inc. World Rights Reserved. Reprinted with special permission of King Features Syndicate. "I Think Therefore I Must Have A Snack" by Pat Miller. Copyright © Pat Miller. Reprinted by permission of the author. "The God" and "My Cup of Tea" by Lillian Morrison. Copyright © 1985 Lillian Morrison. Reprinted by permission of the author. Excerpt from *Mama Day*. Copyright © 1988 by Gloria Naylor. Reprinted by permission of Ticknor & Fields, a Houghton Mifflin Company. All rights reserved. "Mugged" by Leslea Newman from *Sweet Dark Places* (Herbooks). Copyright © 1991 Leslea Newman. Reprinted by permission of the author. "My Life" by Susan Orlean. Copyright © 1990 by Susan Orlean. Originally published in *The New Yorker*. Reprinted by permission of the author and The New Yorker Magazine, Inc. "Little House" by Dorothy Parker copyright © 1933, renewed © 1961 by Dorothy Parker, from *The Portable Dorothy Parker* by Dorothy Parker, Introduction by Brendan Gill. Used by permission of Viking Penguin, a division of Penguin Books USA Inc. "Three Ways to Think about Chocolate" and "For Women Only" by Pamela Pettler from *The Joy of Stress*. Copyright © 1984 Pamela Pettler. Used by permission of the author. Excerpt from *Cecile* by Ruthann Robson copyright © Ruthann Robson. Used by permission of Firebrand Press (Ithaca, New York). "Armed Robbery" by Miriam Sagan from *Cradle and All* (Faber & Faber). Copyright © Mirian Sagan. Used by permission of the author. "Therapy Paranoia" from *Anxiety Attack* (Violet Ink, 1992). Copyright © 1992 by Lorrie Sprecher. Used by permission of the author. "So Many Petite Virginettes Ask..." by Judy Tenuta. Copyright © Judy Tenuta. First published in *Esquire* October 1991. Reprinted courtesy of the Hearst Corporation. Excerpts from *The Search for Signs of Intelligent Life in the Universe* by Jane Wagner. Copyright © 1986 by Jane Wagner, Inc. Reprinted by permission of HarperCollins Publishers. "Song" by Alice Walker from *Houses Make A Landscape Look More Beautiful*. Copyright © 1984 by Alice Walker, reprinted by permission of Harcourt Brace Jovanovich, Inc.

dedicated to my sister Diane

contents

romance

two People who are Asking for trouble

Nicole Hollander

10 Reasons Not To Get Married

1. Life, like a Jane Austen novel, has been known to end with a perfectly orchestrated wedding.
2. Closet space.
3. Throwing a wedding will be dangerously similar to entering into a joint business venture with your mother.
4. You can't even buy a *dress* without exchanging it at least once.
5. *Heartburn,* the book.
6. *Heartburn,* the movie.
7. You like squandering your own money.
8. Having an assortment of men's undergarments strewn across your bedroom floor will no longer be sexy and fun—it will be annoying and gross.
9. Five hundred hand-written thank-you notes.
10. It's taken you twenty-some years to learn to live with your *own* little annoying habits.

Sarah Dunn

Rina Piccolo

Annie Lawson

3

Gail Machlis

A date spent in Hell

Joann Palanker

Reading the Signs: How to Make Shallow Snap Judgements

The trick to successful dating is learning how to interpret the hidden signs, those tiny giveaway gestures that can tell you so much about a person. Train yourself to recognize—and decode—these key "signs."

Woman won't unlock car door for man	Doesn't engage in oral sex
Man gets in car without opening door for woman	No foreplay
Can't hail a cab	Impotent
Insists on going to a brand-new restaurant	Prefers virgins
Insists on going to a brand-new restaurant but gets lost on the way	Is a virgin
Insists on going to romantic, candlelit restaurant	Compulsive Don Juan
Insists on going to homey little cafe with windmill motif	Compulsive Don Quixote
Insists on going to Polynesian bar	Compulsive Don Ho
Wants to go to a French restaurant	Will swallow
Wants to go to a deli	Won't swallow
Uses Sweet n' Low	Wearing falsies

Takes too long deciding what to order	Has trouble reaching orgasm
Orders salad dressing on the side	Will give you hand job but will not go "all the way"
Gives explicit orders to waiter	Will expect incredibly skillful gymnastics in bed
Asks for extra rolls	Will say she's using birth control when she's not, will get pregnant, and sue
Insists on ordering for you, referring to you as "The lady will have. . ."	Thinks you had an orgasm when you didn't
Asks for "The usual"	Insists on missionary position only
Asks what the specials are	Will want you to use handcuffs
Fills up on bread and crackers	Premature ejaculator
Doesn't finish everything on plate	Has already come
Insists on eating some of whatever you ordered	Will make you sleep on wet spot
Changes mind after ordering	Will never call you
Changes table	Nymphomaniac
Drinks decaf	Fakes orgasms (female)
Orders in French	Fakes orgasms (male)
Sends food back	Will sleep with you, brag to all his friends, then try to borrow money
Asks for detailed description of desserts	Needs you to talk dirty during sex

Orders a dessert involving ladyfingers	Wants a hand job
Orders a dessert involving nuts	Castrating bitch
Wants to split dessert	Is dying to get rid of her apartment, move in with you, rearrange all your closets, and take down all your baseball posters
Credit card is refused	Low sperm count
Undertips waiter	Small penis
Undertips parking valet	Small penis
Undertips cabbie	Small penis
Uses toothpick	Is trying to tell you size isn't everything
Removable cassette player in car	Pulls out repeatedly during sex
Cellular-phone in car	Penile implant

Pamela Pettler & Amy Heckerling

Marlan Henley

Nina Paley

9

Dear Michael,

Dear Michael,
   Thank you so much for your ~~nice~~..._{warm}

Dear Michael,
   Thank you so much for your letter about the show. I'm so glad you enjoyed it and my performance. I do remember meeting you afterwards and your kind words then.
   Shit...

Dear Michael,
   Thanks for your note! And glad you enjoyed the show. I remember meeting you, the handsome bearded
   For Chrissake...

Dear Michael,
   Thanks for your note. And glad you enjoyed the show. I remember meeting you and am grateful ~~that you wrote~~ for your ~~praise of~~ comments on my work. It was a challenging show to do. You write of good reviews received for your work in *The Real Thing*. But you say self-criticism makes it difficult to accept others' praise of your work.
   ~~Personally, I lap it up~~
   Certainly that quality will push us to continue growing in the theater.
   Sigh...

Dear Michael,
   Thanks for your note. It's hard to answer it without sounding ~~as~~ pompous ~~as you did~~
   I'm glad you liked the show and my work.
   I do vaguely remember meeting you.
   It wasn't inappropriate of you to write.
   I'm glad you got good reviews in your last show.
   I'm glad you like kids and would like to meet mine.
   I do think the four-hour drive throws an obstacle in the path of getting to know each other.
   Fuck...

Dear Margie,
That guy did write me. The one you said has trouble settling down...
                                                              Taffy Field

Annie Lawson

Jan Eliot

"JULIA SHELF, WOMAN ALONE"

Sharone Einhorn

AS A FINAL BLOW, WHEN JULIA LOOKED UP "ROMANCE" THE DICTIONARY SAID: "ROMANCE: SEE UNTRUTH."

Jennifer Camper

The relationship was taking its toll on
Louba's confidence.

SYLVIA

Nicole Hollander

Stephanie Piro

She was suddenly reminded of the time she made Barbie dump Ken and move in with G.I. Joe...

Dykes To Watch Out For

Allison Bechdel

Jan Eliot

Grounded in Reality:
An Affair with Superman
that Never Took Off

A strange set of coincidences happened to me recently. Every time I turned on my television, not only was the same rerun of the movie "Superman" playing on cable but the same scene. It's the one in which Superman grants Lois Lane an interview on her terrace and then takes her flying above New York City. It is ever so romantic. On the ground there is preliminary banter between them, notably a cute remark by Superman about the color of Lois' underwear, courtesy of his X-Ray vision. Then the two have their climactic romp in the heavens.

Seeing the same sequence three times got me caught up in the fantasy. As I went about my daily activities I found I was mentally substituting myself for Lois Lane. The repetition had given me the opportunity to memorize all the dialogue and visualize most of the gliding patterns.

Last night I had a frustrating dream. In it Superman dropped down to my patio to whisk me away, but we never made it past my kitchen. Just as Peter Pan couldn't take the grown-up Wendy to Never-Never Land, I, the mother of two teenaged children, couldn't get off the ground with Superman.

I detoured from the storyline just before Superman and I are about to take off and I say I will get my sweater, like Lois did. In the movie Superman says she won't need it, and Lois gives a carefree smile or perhaps a smirk. The implication is that Superman will keep her warm. In my dream I tell Superman, "The only way I'd feel secure flying with you is if I'd get sweaters for both of us, 'just in case.'" It did occur to me that Superman wouldn't be able to get a sweater on over his cape; I wanted to nurture him.

From then, everything became complicated. I decided to forget the sweater and instead change out of Lois' chiffon dress and into a whole other outfit. She may have been able to keep the dress smooth and flowing in flight, but my experience with silk nightgowns told me that after the first downwind, the dress would end up around my neck. I quickly got into a pair of slacks, socks and gym shoes and a hooded sweatshirt. Then I remembered it would be best to layer the sweatshirt over a knit shirt, so I changed again. I reasoned I could always tie the sweatshirt around my waist if I got too warm when I was flying.

In one of the pockets I stuffed facial tissue in case my nose ran at high altitudes. Then I remembered how my hair reacted in the wind, so I went to my daughter's drawer and got a few barrettes to anchor it. Next I put a note out for the kids and left them money to order a pizza.

Before I rejoined Superman, my girlfriend Sharon called, and I couldn't resist telling her about my impending adventure. I decided that to keep Superman occupied while I was on the phone, I'd reheat some Chinese food for him in the microwave.

I got off the phone and took a look at myself and realized I was dressed like a camp counselor. Superman peered up from his plate and gave me an adoring look. He wanted another helping. With resignation I joined him at the table, and the two of us chatted about intimate things: his yearning for Krypton and my fear of heights. Together we finished off the rest of the stir-fry.

Susan Chertkow

Nicole Hollander

Gail Machlis

Good Vibrations

About a month ago, I was shown some products designed to
improve the sex lives of suburban housewives. I got so
excited,
I just had to come on public access and tell you about it. To
look at *me*, you'd *never suspect* I was a semi-nonorgasmic
woman. This means it was *possible* for me to have an orgasm—
but highly unlikely.

To me, the term "sexual freedom" meant freedom from having to
have sex. And then along came Good Vibrations. And was I
surprised! Now I am a regular
Cat on a Hot Tin Roof.

As a love object,
it surpasses my husband Harold by a country mile.
But please,
this is no threat to the family unit;
think of it as a kind of
Hamburger Helper for the boudoir.

Can you afford one, you say?
Can you afford not to have one, I say.
Why, the time it saves alone is worth the price.
I'd rank it up there with Minute Rice,
Reddi-Wip
and Pop-Tarts.

Ladies, it simply takes the guesswork out of making love.

"But doesn't it kill romance?" you say.
And I say,
"What doesn't?"

So what'll it be? This deluxe kit? Or this purse-size model
for the "woman on the go"? Fits anywhere and comes with a
silencer to avoid
curious onlookers.

Ladies, it can be a real help to the busy married woman who has a thousand chores and simply does not need the extra burden of trying to have an orgasm.

But what about guilt, you say? Well, that thought did cross my mind.

But at one time I felt guilty using a cake mix instead of baking from scratch.

I learned to live with that.
I can learn to live with this.

Jane Wagner
excerpt from *The Search for Signs of Intelligent Life in the Universe*

The next day at the office Mary thanked
everyone for the surprise party.

The Day the Dog Ran Away with My Survival Dick

Foolishly, and probably due to my recently achieved euphoria, I left the bottom bedside table drawer open by a fractional crack. I am usually very careful, especially where my buddy, delightful dick, is concerned. I guard the secret of his existence with the utmost discretion.

Anyway, this fine and sunny morning, while I was in the shower and hubby was at work, my dog labored industriously, widening the crack in the drawer until her nose fit in to explore. *Aha! What's this? Looks interesting,* she thought, as she feverishly and hurriedly began wiggling her soft, pink prize out of the drawer. Almost succeeding, she cocked her head as she heard the shower door slide open. *Hurry,* her little mischievous brain prompted. With one last tug she freed my best friend and dove under the bed with her treasure. Poor dick. I should tell you that the thief was a toy poodle and my friend was all of 8" long and 2" thick, a realistic replica of the real thing.

Completely unaware, I had breakfast, with the thief no less, her trophy well hidden. Let me interject an explanation to what you are probably wondering. Why would I have the need of survival dick when I had a husband? The latter was physically equipped, to be sure. He had even fathered three children. That's where it stopped, having to do, I suppose, with the Biblical admonishment that sex was for procreation purposes. He was convinced that God-fearing man was not meant to indulge in sex for any other purpose. So be it.

Back to dick. After breakfast, little Frenchy decided to claim her prize. She held doleful dick sideways in her mouth in a firm grip, head held high so as not to drag it. Heavens, no! Her treasure. As she paraded proudly past me, I gave her an innocent, indulgent chuckle. Wait a minute! I did a double take and my blood froze. Just then the front door popped open and my good friend and neighbor strode in. I screamed, "Don't let her out!" to my startled friend. Too late. Through the door, lickety split and down the walk at a good clip.

"We *have* to catch her," I ordered as I pulled Judy after me through the door.

"You're not dressed!"

"Too late to worry about that now. Hurry! She's halfway up the street already," I shrieked.

Panting and in pursuit, Judy asked, "What does she have?"

"My dildo."

Judy stopped short, her mouth hanging open. "Your...?"

She was laughing so hard she sank down on the curb, holding her sides. Her uproarious laughter was lost in the distance as I dashed on in pursuit of poodle and pacifier.

Two streets further I lost sight of her on a corner. "Oh, God!" Now I was only worried about my little poodle. I started yelling at anyone I could find, "My dog. Have you seen my small, black poodle run by?"

"That way, lady."

There she was! I sprinted the last few hundred feet. Just before I reached her, a well built man blocked her escape route. His big hand grabbed her by the scruff of her neck and held her aloft. Delightful dick was still protruding from both sides of her firmly clasped mouth.

I saw the incredulous expression on the handsome rescuer's face change to one of glee. As the curious drew near, he held my poodle upside down and quickly and efficiently caught dick as it dropped from the dog's mouth. Deftly, he slipped Dick under his MacGregor jacket.

I grabbed my poodle, mumbled a "thank you," and did a brisk walk all the way back home. I never even gave my faithful friend, delightful dick, a farewell glance. I gathered my convulsed friend from the curb and locked all of us in the house.

Saved! Do you think so?

Two days later the hero rescuer was standing at my door, a 9" x 3" box cradled under his arm. There was a grin on his face a mile wide. But that's another story.

Johanna

Sharone Einhorn

UP UNTIL NOW, SIZE HAD NOT BEEN A
MAJOR CONSIDERATION FOR MRS. LEBLANC.

Fortune Reading...In Bed

After seven years of living in Chinatown, I can tell you with some authority the proper way to read a fortune cookie.

To divine the true meaning of your squib, you must know that there are always two words omitted at the end: "in bed." For example:

"He that falls in love with himself will have no rivals"...in bed.

"A handful of patience is worth more than a bushel of brains"...in bed

"Life is a tragedy for those who feel and a comedy for those who think"...in bed.

Flash Rosenberg

I Was Thinking of Sex

I was thinking of sex when a horn blared and a taxicab screeched to a stop beside me at a red light.

"Fucking bitch!" the driver yelled fiercely at me.

"It's idiots like you that make the roads unsafe!"

"Cram it, buddy!" I yelled back. "I don't know what the hell you're talking about!"

"Goddamn idiot! You swerved right in front of me! You weren't paying attention at all! Could have killed us both, lady! They should keep people like you off the roads!"

"Hah!" I yelled back. "You were probably going too damned fast and now you're trying to blame it on me! It's a wonder there's anyone left alive in this city with all you fucking cab drivers speeding around the way you do!"

We were both red in the face. The light turned green. We were still glaring at each other. Suddenly he broke into a beautiful smile. "Hey. . . have a nice day!" he said.

"You, too!" I smiled back.

We drove off. I was no longer thinking about sex.

Joan Tollifson

excerpt from *Watering The Plants*

Jan Eliot

As usual, Rona's husband wasn't
really listening to her.

Andrea Natalie

It was the first and last time McClain
and Schwartz would forget to
turn off the intercom.

Andrea Natalie

A Woman Tells Men:

Everything You've Always Wanted to Know About Women and Probably Won't Understand When I Explain It to You

First of all, women want more sex than you do. They want it more often, with more variation of technique, and they want it to last longer than you can possible bear. They also want it wilder, louder, and messier than you can ever imagine.

Even though you have been taught that women do not want to have sex as much as you do and women were taught that they shouldn't want it as much as you, you should not be surprised when you are lying in bed, besieged by financial worries and exhausted by a long day at work, and your girlfriend, who is every bit as exhausted and besieged as you are, is humping your thigh suggestively and running her fingers through your chest hair. You will go sleep on the couch and she will feel rejected and the relationship will fall apart soon after you come home and find her in bed with another guy.

There is probably nothing you can do about this sad state of affairs, but at least now you will know

—what made her cry.

—what she meant when she said she needed more of your time.

—what she's telling all her girlfriends about you. (He withheld sex.)

—why she slept with your brother who is still in high school.

Because women are never able to get as much sex as they need, almost everything they do is for the purpose of sexual sublimation.

Shopping is big with women who aren't getting enough sex. It's physically very tiring and involves a lot of undressing in front of mirrors. It is best performed in the company of another equally horny woman who says things like "If it feels good, buy it." Spending large sums of money induces the same exquisite feelings of guilt that we associate with spicy sex.

Eating is the ideal obsession for the sex-starved woman. Every fat woman you see is not getting enough sex. Every thin woman you see is passionately trying to whittle herself down to the shape of an underdeveloped and sexually nonthreatening twelve-year-old girl in hopes that she will be able to attract men and get more sex.

Men do their best to make a woman believe that the reason they don't want to have sex is because there is something wrong with her. This keeps women off their backs and caught up on a global hamster-wheel of self-improvement. It's also great for the guys who are selling health club memberships. Many women have found that strenuous exercise is a good way to fool your body into thinking it has just had sex.

Fat or thin, women's lives tend to revolve around food—the preparation of it, the consumption of it, and, most fondly, the avoidance of it. These days, the only way to be a wanton woman is to eat half a dozen cookies for breakfast.

Public speaking, driving small foreign cars, and standing in line at the bank are all typical forms of female sexual sublimation. In fact, for many women, disappointing sex is itself a substitute for something better, yet unobtainable.

Men are particularly attracted to women who look as if they can't have sex. These women wear tight clothing, uncomfortable shoes, stiff hair, and lots of makeup that shouldn't be messed up. They frequently die an early death from inhaling too much hair spray, or they commit suicide because they can't figure out why, if they look so yummy, they can't get that dreamboat into the sack more often.

You have probably always thought that men like women who refuse to go to bed with them on the first date because it means that they are discriminating. Wrong. What men like is a woman who is either extremely sexually repressed or has a great deal of self-control. That's the only kind of woman a man can stand to be around for any length of time. Otherwise, he runs the risk of her trying to stroke his crotch at unusual hours or offering oral sex while he's trying to concentrate on spectator sports.

So most women hold off on that first date, hoping to appear discriminating, which they aren't. (And if you don't believe me, just check out the bodies of the men most women go out with.) Then they will marry the guy, hoping to ensure a steady supply of sex.

These women soon sour and turn into the kind of hard-lipped unsatisfied bitches that James M. Cain made famous —ready to kill their husbands and frame their lovers as well.

Women constantly complain that men are unable to sustain relationships. Give me a break. Men do fine in relationships where there is no sex. Take your parents, for instance. You don't really think they were able to find a way to have sex without your knowing it, do you? You were right all along. Your parents didn't fuck.

"Giving her a baby" is one of guys' favorite ways of keeping women occupied with something other than fooling around in the bedroom. At least until the kids are old enough to go to school and she can spend her afternoons next door trying to seduce the neighbor who got laid off six months ago and can't find another job so his wife had to go to work. This will probably motivate him to accept the next job offer that comes along even if he is way overqualified. And when an adulterous liaison is formed, it is only so that the man can avoid having sex with two women at the same time. He tells the lover he has to spend time with his wife and justifies his lack of interest in his wife by having something going on the side.

Here is a typical plot: The guy just has to go out and selflessly risk his life to stop the crazy sniper/terrorist/mad-dog/cornered bank robber/kidnapper. His wife pleads with him not to go and suggests that he stay home and they'll give each other blowjobs instead.

The woman is portrayed as a selfish slut.

The guy is a hero.

He dodges the gunman's bullets, climbs a vine to the top of the tower/bunker/embattled embassy/machine gun nest, confronts the bad guy face to face, overpowers him but is wounded in the struggle, becomes a quadriplegic, and his wife has to spoonfeed him for the rest of his life. Eventually a statue is erected on the site to commemorate his heroism. The guy has managed to avoid sex on a full-time basis.

Men trip over each other rushing to live out this scenario.

Over the ages, men have been able to glorify the most awful shit in the world in order to disguise the fact that they're only using it as an excuse to avoid having sex with women. Face it, guys, going to bed with a woman is a hell of a lot scarier than marching into an enemy mine field. The worst thing that can happen in war is that you die. If you screw up in bed with a woman, she will tell you and everybody else who will listen what a fool you were. She'll laugh at you and make funny little gestures that indicate the size and shape of your weenie. And you can only *wish* you were dead.

Why take the chance?

But men have to be cool and pretend that they have nothing to worry about even though vaginas are hot and dark and gooshy and you're expected to put the most precious part of your body in there. No wonder you need massive amounts of drugs, alcohol, and emotional detachment in order to do it.

I'd like to clear one last thing up before I go off and eat an entire banana cream pie all by myself: Men and women do not get stuck together like dogs when they screw.

Oh, sure. You can beat her at arm wrestling, throw her across the room, mow her down in the line for Bruce Springsteen tickets, but you're no match for her vagina? Come on.

If a woman could keep you inside her by clamping her vaginal muscles in an inextricable viselike grip, you'd be there now.

Shary Flenniken

Shary Flenniken

A Sunday Night at a Drug Store

I, a very bashful woman, was out with an even more bashful man buying a condom. As with most products these days, there are too many varieties to choose from: latex or animal skin, ribbed or plain, spermicide-coated, lubricated, day-glow colored—and all the permutations and combinations. If, we speculated, you were to weigh all the pros and cons of what these options permitted, the desire for sex would subside—this was the *real* method by which they prevent pregnancy. We chose a box of lubricated Lady Trojans—on sale for $3.59. At my neighborhood drug store in Washington, D.C., all condoms come in the twelve-pack.

The cashier seemed slower than a D.C. snow plow. She had a glazed expression, and after tallying purchases she flashed a look that said: "You ought to be grateful I'm willing to take your money at all." As we came to the head of the line she snapped: "That'll be $7.59."

"Excuse me," I said—"I think you overcharged us. The sign on the shelf says '$3.59.'"

She pulled our package over the scanner. "Nah, the orgy size twelve-pack is $7.16," she snorted and started ringing up the next customers, a pair of nuns.

Feeling the sisters' eyes boring into my back, I said: "I'm positive they're $3.59." The clerk sighed and spoke in to a microphone. "Register three requesting a price check on Lady Trojans *twelve*-pack," she boomed. As her questions echoed between the aisles, what little urges we had left vanished. Behind us stood a punk with hair as pink as the box of condoms. The cashier rang up his Sassoon conditioner and boomed into the microphone: "Register three waiting on a price check on Lady's Trojans *twelve*-pack, the *lubricated* kind." The punk said: "My girl, she likes the ones with ribs. You should've got them." I was grateful we hadn't, and especially grateful we hadn't settled on some in day-glow colors.

At last the cashier asked a security guard to go check the price.

"Lady Trojans in a *twelve*-pack, *lubricated*, $3.65!" a voice bellowed over the loudspeaker a moment later. I was beginning to think the nun's celibate life might really be for me. Fondling the box, the cashier said: "Hmmph." It was the first time she had showed a spark of life.

"Perhaps she's in need of a cheap box of condoms in numbers sufficient for an orgy," I remarked to the nuns. But they had vanished. Glancing up, I noticed the nuns scurrying down the condom aisle.

Theresa McCracken

Ros Asquith

AT THE STROKE OF MIDNIGHT, CINDERELLA'S PUSSY TURNS INTO A PUMPKIN. AS SHE HURRIES TO LEAVE THE BALL, SHE RUNS INTO THE HANDSOME PRINCE.

Kris Kovick

shoe thing

LIKE SO MANY OTHER WOMEN, SHE HAD A WEAKNESS FOR SHOES.

...AND THE SWEETEST PAIR OF BLUE LIZARD PUMPS!

AND LIKE SO MANY, SHE COULD NEVER BRING HERSELF TO THROW ANYTHING AWAY.

SO THE DISCARDED SHOES PILED UP IN HER CLOSET.

SOMETIMES OTHER REJECTS FOUND THEIR WAY ONTO THE PILE.

OOH! IT'S "BITCH IN HEAT" MUSK OIL! MY (Ugh!) FAVORITE!

YUCK!

IT BECAME A GOOD PLACE FOR THE CAT TO PEE.

A DRESS, UNWORN FOR THREE YEARS, FELL ONTO THE PILE.

THEN, ON THE HOTTEST DAY OF THE YEAR...

THE MOLDERING SHOES, SATURATED WITH MUSK OIL AND CAT PEE, HEATED TO BODY TEMPERATURE...

...SLOWLY STIRRED AND TOOK SHAPE.

THUS WAS FORMED...

SHOE THING

GOOD LORD! ≥CHOKE≤

by Trina Robbins

Lettered by L. Lois Buhalis

TOTTERING ON PLATFORM SOLES, IT SHUFFLED THROUGH THE HUMID SUMMER NIGHT...

...TO EMERGE FROM THE FOG, HOURS LATER, IN FRONT OF FERN'S SINGLE CITY, 15 MINUTES BEFORE CLOSING TIME.

BAR & GRILL

IT STAGGERED IN, ON ROPE-SOLED WEDGIES.

Trina Robbins

breaking up

Jennifer Berman

Annie Lawson

Marian Henley

All she had left of the
relationship were his used
cigarette butts which she
held close to her nose
to preserve his smell
in her memory.

Mary Lawton

Barbara Brandon

Kathleen DeBold

madonna at the mall (pop culture)

Chris Suddick

The American Woman Rag

Apparently it is written in some little-read corner of the Constitution that the most foul, the most vile, the most icksome products of American society shall be prominently displayed at the check-out counters of supermarkets all across this great nation of ours. Because the other day, there among *The National Enquirer, The Star* and the Breath Mints Made From 100% Proven Carcinogens, I spied a newcomer—a magazine called *American Woman.* And since I am one, I bought a copy. Here is what I got for my $1.99:

Cover

A model who looks like a real person, only more like a model. Juicy cover lines such as: *Sexual Ecstasy, 8 Strategies For Meeting A New Lover! and Lose 5 Lbs. By Monday Morning.*

Articles

They're mostly about how to look more like a model and act more like a walking, talking vagina so that men will want to have sex with you. I had no idea it was so difficult to get men to have sex, but I guess I'm naive. Anyway, there are also several really serious articles for the really serious American (Career) Woman, such as *On the Job: Coping, Cavorting from 9 to 5.* Here I found hot career tips such as: I can "cash in" by giving "parties" at which I pressure my "friends" into buying cheap jewelry, cooking utensils, cleaning supplies and, if they're *really* stupid, the 8 stained-glass-look jelly jars my Aunt Bea gave me for the hope chest. Plus: *6 Ways to Pounce on Paper Pileups.* See the American Woman pounce! Pounce, pounce, American Woman! Cavort, cavort!

Another article on happening careers suggests that the American Woman would be right at home in Child Care or Public Relations, which I'm sure you've never heard before if you've been having sex nonstop since 1957, which is the true meaning of success according to American Woman. In that case, you'll also be surprised to hear that *jeans are in right now.*

And before we leave the fashion arena, there are *10 Things You Must Have for Fall,* including Schoolgirl Charm, Cute Boots and Plenty of Plaid!!! The writer doesn't come right out and say that the idea is to look as much like a 12-year-old nymphomaniac as you possibly can, but it comes across.

But enough about careers and clothes and other sideshows of life. Let's talk about sex. The first thing the American Woman needs in order to have sex is a man—any man. Among the *8 Sure-Fire Man-Meeting Strategies* offered by writers Sharyn Wolf and Katy Koontz, who are obviously experts at this sort of thing:

• *Bar hop.* (Remember, you've been in bed since 1957, so you've never heard of bar-hopping, much less herpes, psycho killers or AIDS.)

•*Walk a dog.* And here's the touch of genius: It doesn't have to be *your* dog —you can borrow one from someone who actually likes animals, and use it as bait! (One thing the writers didn't mention: You could actually try to find out the dog's name, in case a man says he will have sex with you if you know what it is! I thought of that myself, so obviously I'm learning to think like a real American Woman!) Thank God these fine minds didn't get sidetracked into some puny career like brain surgery, where they could help only a few hundred people, instead of millions of American Women.

•*Shop in a men's store.* It's so obvious, I don't know how I could have overlooked it myself. You need a man, you go to a store that sells ... *men!!!*

But, you know, if you're like me, sometimes when you do find a man in your house, you don't quite know what to do with him. Well, Ellen Kreidman knows what you and I don't: "Become a woman who is indispensable to your man and his self-image, and you will be a woman to whom a man feels passionately and hopeless in love with."

Now, you may have noticed, as I did, that that sentence is the grammatical equivalent of scrambled eggs. But, hey, if you and I had as much sex as the American Woman, we probably wouldn't be able to string together a sentence, either. In fact, a functioning brain could be a sign of insufficient cavorting! In any case, it's no use whatsoever in the heat of a manhunt.

In addition to being a woman to whom a man feels passionately and hopelessly in love with, you may have to do a few other little things, as well, if you want a guy to stick around for repeat performances. An article called *Light His Fire: 7 Red-Hot Ways to Keep Him Burning With Desire,* suggests that you "forget" to put silverware on the table, so you're both forced to eat with your hands, which causes sex. (Note the emphasis on forgetting—another gentle hint that a guy wants his American Woman to be sharp as a marble.)

Now I see that I've been doing this all wrong, because I generally tell men I "forgot" to buy groceries and we'll have to eat out. And, sure enough, I have to wait until after dinner to have sex every time. But hey, I guess I'm lucky I get any at all, seeing as how I *forgot* to *stock up on red light bulbs.*

That brings us to the Special Section, entitled —you won't be shocked —*Are You Good In Bed?* But never mind, it's actually an excerpt from The Kinsey Institute New Report on Sex, written by a couple of researchers whose grammatically correct, slightly clinical prose seems to indicate that they should stop researching so much and just do it until their brains melt. Either the Special Section should have been called: *Thoughtful Health Professionals Answer Your Questions About Sex,* or it should have been written by some of the regular writers who really know how to write stuff to whom a reader feels passionately and hopelessly in love with.

Advertisements

With the generous, caring help of the many, many companies that have thoughtfully explained their breakthrough, miracle products to readers of *American Woman*, I can whiten my teeth; beautify *and* boost my bust; end acne; free myself of ugly veins; get stronger, richer, thicker, longer hair; a smoother, softer, younger-looking complexion; and lose 30 pounds in 30 days without dieting and no exercise! Of course, if I lose 30 pounds I'll weigh 77 pounds, but that is just about what I weighed when I was 12, and if my hair were longer and my skin were smoother, softer, younger-looking, I might actually pass for 12, which would be really bitchin'.

Notes and Comment

Okay, in all seriousness, perhaps you are wondering: Who would publish 80-plus pages of degrading, bee-brained, retro-sleaze and add insult to idiocy by calling it *American Woman?* Well, his name is Charles Goodman, and he may be an American, but I'll bet he ain't a Woman. And if you ain't a 12-year-old, chronically confused nymphomaniac, you may find that you want a little more respect than you get from Chuck's rag. So, leave it there at the check-out stand along with the other toxic waste materials of a sick society, and go buy *The Color Purple* or *To Kill a Mockingbird* or even *Gone With the Wind* —all written by *real* American Women. Of course, you won't find them at the check-out stand, and maybe not even in your bookstore or library, because they've all been banned at one time or another.

Go figure.

Candyce Meherani

Madonna & Me

With not one but *three* biographies of Madonna hitting the stores this month, it's presumably not news to you that Madonna used to shock everyone in high school by vaulting to the top of her cheerleader pyramid without any underwear on.

She was wearing fleshcolored tights. But from a distance—to a person sitting midway up the stands behind the band (the geeks) —Madonna was every teenage boy's fantasy: a cheerleader who forgot to put on her underpants.

Of course, Marilyn Monroe would have forgotten her underpants— Madonna *chose* not to wear them. And she would go on to build a career by willfully and flagrantly violating one of my mother's cardinal rules (always wear the appropriate undergarments). What's more, she would eventually get an entire generation to follow suit. Anyone who caught Madonna on *Nightline*, defending her "Justify My Love" video, got a sense of the Madonna that the biographers have been trying so hard to pin down:

"I have chained myself. There wasn't a man that put that chain on me. I did it myself. I was chained to my desires. I crawled under my own table, you know? There wasn't a man standing there making me do it. I do everything of my own volition. I'm in charge."

Now, I can't go so far as to claim to have put on my own chains. To be totally honest, I don't even have any chains lying around that I *could* don, as a political statement or otherwise. What with the new Kryptonite bike lock thing, who does? And even if I *did*, I'd probably ask myself, "Yeah. But what's the *point.*"

Still, as I read through Christopher Andersen's *Madonna: Unauthorized,* I was struck by a slew of uncanny coincidences. Kind of like I was reading my own biography. Not just the little things (I like popcorn; my slip often shows; I'm really not all that talented) but some major, parallel universe type of occurrences that make me wonder if maybe I might actually be Madonna:

MADONNA: Recently divorced from Sean Penn.
ME: Recently graduated from U. Penn.
MADONNA: Willing to work for union scale, $1,440 a week (essentially for free), to land the part as Breathless Mahoney in order to further her acting career.
ME: Willing to work for $2.35 an hour (essentially for free) as a waitress in order to further my writing career.
MADONNA: Claims all of her earliest sexual experiences were with

females. Hobnobs with the openly bisexual Sandra Bernhard, hugging, cradling, and kissing her in public; visits such lesbian bars as the Cubby Hole.

ME: Some of my closest friends are women; had a cubby hole assigned to me in kindergarten.

MADONNA: Often found cruising the Lower East Side of New York in a limousine, picking up banji boys for cheap and meaningless sexual encounters, then casting them aside like so many used pieces of Kleenex.

ME: Wisely limit my cheap and meaningless sexual encounters to those whom *no one would find credible* if they were ever to come forward.

MADONNA: Decision to pursue classical dance was altered by the realization that it would take three to five years for her to earn a spot with a major touring dance company.

ME: Decision to pursue classical dance was altered when forced to appear in early ballet recital dressed as a chicken.

MADONNA: As a youth, would frequently attend church wearing nothing under her overcoat.

ME: As a youth, would frequently attend church.

MADONNA: Visitors to her Hollywood Hills house often comment on the depiction of male genitals covering Madonna's living room ceiling.

ME: Visitors to my Center City apartment often comment on the excessively long, thin hallway that culminates in a distinctively "womb-like" living room.

MADONNA: As a young girl, enlisted her naked Barbie dolls to act out her sexual fantasies.

ME: As a young girl, enlisted my naked Barbie dolls to act out my sexual fantasies.

MADONNA: Seduced more than 100 men between her arrival in New York in 1979 and her first hit record in 1983.

ME: Was *nowhere near* New York between 1979 and 1983, for your information, Mother.

Of course, they teach an entire course on Madonna at Harvard. I can't compete with that. Or the 200 million dollar personal empire thing. And I've never had a man throw his underwear at my feet in a public "come hither" type gesture...

So don't mind me. I'm just going to go practice crawling under my *own* table, you know?

Sarah Dunn

SHE WAS SO OBSESSED WITH MADONNA
SHE TRIPPED OVER THE BED AND FELL OUT THE WINDOW

Diane Dimassa

Mall-o-Genesis

In the beginning, God created the Heavens and the earth. The earth was without form and was empty. It was uncivilized, crude, lacked uniformity and you couldn't find a light bulb anywhere. God said, 'Let there be light' and there was Fluorescence. God saw that it was good and He separated light from the darkness. God called the light 'day' and there was no darkness because He put in twenty-four hour lighting that stayed on even after hours. And there was evening and morning. The first Shopping day.

The second day, He said, 'Let there be a sky light on the top floor.' Then He put in a row of designer luxury ice cream Stores and a Godiva chocolate Store. He called this Heaven.

The third day, God said, 'Let all the Consumer Products everywhere be gathered together in one place under one roof.' And it was so. God called this lighted, perfect place 'Mall,' and the rest of the world, well, the rest of the world no longer existed. And God said, 'Let Mall bring forth plastic palm trees and let chlorinated waterfalls and pools flow freely in the courtyards in front of the Exotic Bath Supply Store. Mall did so and God saw that it was good. This was the third Shopping day.

The fourth day, God said, 'Let there be more track lighting in the third floor so we can see all the beauty and behold the United Colors of Benetton.'

The fifth day, God said, 'Let the Sales bring in great numbers of moving creatures that have life, many women to Sell things and to clean things. So God created the Saleswoman and every living creature that moves. He saw the janitors and security people move in great numbers, and saw that all this was good.

The sixth day, God said, 'Let Mall bring forth Commodities of all kinds. Let us Sell Products in our own American image, let Mall have power over the fish of the sea, and over every local culture of the world.' And so God created the international food Emporium.

Thus, God created the Mall Shopper in His own image. And He blessed them and said to them, 'Be silent, fruitful and multiply. Consume the earth and have power over every other people and over nature itself. Behold, I have given you white spongy bread, pizza-size chocolate chip cookies and plenty of hamburgers.' And it was so. God saw everything He had made, and it was very good. This was the sixth Shopping day.

The seventh day, Mall was complete and was teeming with Shoppers. On the seventh day, God rested from His work and all that He had made but hardly anyone else did because there were only thirty-four Shopping days left till Christmas and everybody was working seven days a week plus overtime. But the big deal Executives did rest, they made the seventh day a holy day, because on that day they lounged around and drank Poland Spring in their jacuzzis.

This is how the Lord God made Mall, and each of the five Heavenly floors, and every plastic plant, and every rack of polyester and the indoor waterfall, and the glass elevator that went up and down. And when God had made the Shopper, a mist had gone up from the earth, and God formed the Shopper from the dust in the parking lot, and had breathed into Him the breath of life, and the Shopper became a living soul.

Chaia Zbloki Heller

Jennifer Berman

Take Two Screams and Call me in the Morning

"Express your emotions,"
Most doctors say—
"You'll avoid ulcers
And headaches that way."

So, when I am angry,
I slam doors and yell.
I'M FINE!
(But my family's
Not feeling too well.)

Annie Komorny

Mary Lawton

Annie Lawson

Armed Robbery

The day I held up the 7-11 I was in a bad mood. I had morning sickness until late afternoon and there was nothing to eat in the house. The heat of late June lay over the bad end of town. I lay on the couch reading *From Russia With Love* and drinking flat ginger ale without ice. Then I took the gun out of the shoe box where it sat on top of a pair of red Italian sandals with dirty heels. I took the gun, got into the truck, drove down Agua Fria, and parked outside the 7-11. I could have simply taken a $20 bill out of my underwear drawer but I was in no mood to go shopping. I walked into the 7-11 tripping over my flip flops. My armpits smelled of dust. Inside I put the gun on the counter. "This is a hold-up," I said to the lady behind the counter. She was a Spanish lady of about 50. Her name tag read: Maureen. "What's your problem?" said Maureen. "I'm going to have a baby," I said peevishly. "Does that give you the right to come busting in here?" she said. "I'm a wreck," I said. "I should have gotten my Ph.D. in English literature like my mother wanted me to." "Shit," said Maureen. "You think you're the first woman in the world to have a baby? Calm down girl. You'll feel a lot better when you get into the second trimester. Right now your hormones are just going wild." "And I'm sick to my stomach all the time." "Crackers," said Maureen. "You need crackers." She pulled down a box of saltines for me. Then she opened a can of Diet Pepsi for herself and poured me a glass of apple juice. "I can't pay for this you know," I said. "That's alright," said Maureen. "Consider it part of the hold-up."

Miriam Sagan

Joann Palanker

laughter

Just like a Woman

J.E. Randall

Roberta Gregory

SYLVIA

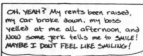

EXPERTS SAY THAT WOMEN SMILE 50% MORE THAN MEN.

10-28

PROBABLY because we HAVE SO MUCH MORE to SMILE About.

MA, WHAt does it MEAN WHEN the PHONE BiLL COMES ON RED PAPER?

©1990 BY NICOLE HOLLANDER

Nicole Hollander

Posy Simmonds

He suffered from one of Man's
Most basic fears . . . fear of
Laughing Women . . .

Stephanie Piro

Flash Rosenberg

HOW TO LAUGH WHILE WEARING LIPSTICK, SO THAT NO SMEARING ON TEETH OCCURS.

1. Listen to joke.

...so the guy goes to use the toilet and while he's there...

2. Plan how hard you want to laugh.

It wasn't **THAT** funny.

3. Gently stretch lips over teeth, AND delicately point tongue upward to touch top lip.

4. Make SMALL, SQUEAKY INWARD gasps, in Rapid SUCCESSION, WHILE keeping this position.

HEH-HEH-HEH-HEH-HEH-HEH!!

5. WHEN Laughter stops, Lipstick AND teeth SHOULD BE PERFECTLY INTACT.

NEXT: HOW TO PREVENT MASCARA FROM DRIPPING WHILE LAUGHING HYSTERICALLY.

Mary Lawton

Nicole Hollander

War, Work and Worry

Before the war started, a friend of mine proposed that Bush and Hussein go off to a small room together. I figured she'd say that the two of them should just slug it out. But no, she suggested that they go into the room, close the door, pull down their pants, and compare penis sizes. Whoever's was bigger would be declared the winner and everybody could go home.

Ellen Orleans

Sharon Rudahl

Kris Kovick

Chris Suddick

Wars of the Mind

There's nothing like a war to bring up all those ugly-little-things-you're-not-supposed-to-be-thinking.

People will say one thing in a living room, among friends; another thing, carefully, in public.

Take: The Weaponry Nomenclature Issue.

Some Higher Power obviously decided in advance who in this conflict would get to use all the weapons with the good, high-minded sounding names. ("OK, you guys in the white hats get the 'Patriots.' And you guys with the greasy black mustaches get the 'Scuds.'")

A part of you responds viscerally to this. And a part wonders: Who decides these things? ("Why don't we develop a missile called the 'Freedom of Expression'? And we'll call their missile the 'Bleccch.' The 'P-tooooey.'")

Then there's The Hotdog-Newsman-Obviously-Gunning-for-a-Pulitzer-Issue.

Each day, it seems, someone in the news media tries to outdo his colleagues; putting himself at some kind of needless risk. ("Yes, here I am doing a handstand on the roof of the Baghdad Hilton, and I have a tiny microphone attached to my left shoe...")

And related to this there is The Daily, Painfully-Obvious Serviceman's Family Question.

Somebody on one of the four major networks, at least once a day, manages to rope a serviceman's family into an on-camera interview, so that the question can be asked: "What does it 'feel' like at a time like this?" (The jackpot answer would be, "It's a day at the beach, Tom. We love this thing so much, we just hope it drags on forever.")

I won't deny it, though, that something did happen those first few days, no question, that horrified a lot of us who grew up in the '60s; who took it as an article of faith that wars were always something you protested. Something that Worked Badly. Something that made people sorrowful.

For at least the first 48 hours, the whole business was actually, well, (gulp) kind of fun. It was 3-D Nintendo-with-a-Vengeance. Literally.

It was living proof that sometimes, in massive Middle Eastern military actions, Murphy's Law refuses to function. Things, inexplicably, Work Right. We find ourselves with our dove feathers flaking off noticeably: "Did you hear that one of those suckers, fired in pitch-darkness, could hit a Winnebago parked in Cincinnati?"

The correct social ("home-front") attitude seems to be, "I don't like this business one little bit. Although, if it was a movie, I would buy tickets to it. It's got a good script, and the characters are one-dimensional and alluring."

Except, of course, we'd feel differently if the movie screen would actually shoot back.

Stephanie Brush

World Leader Pyjamas

"Air Offensive" "Ground Offensive" "The General Massacre"

Sleep well fellas!

Judy Horacek

War Hero

after his victory
     300,000 Iraqis
     killed by the U.S.

Stormin' Norman
aims high

a book deal
could bring a
$4 million advance
topped with
lecture circuit bucks
     he could command
     $60,000 per speech

so he declines the
President's offer
     Army Chief of Staff

that would be
overkill
       Ellen Mark

N. Leigh Dunlap

WORKED UP

BY LYNDA "GEORGE + SADDAM = TRUE LOVE" BARRY ©91

WAR! UH! GOOD GOD Y'ALL! WHAT IS IT GOOD FOR! MY SISTER MARLYS KEPT SINGING THAT SONG AT RECESS. HER TEACHER SAID STOP. MARLYS SAID IT'S A FREE COUNTRY. HER TEACHER CALLED OUR GRANDMA. IT IS NOT A FREE COUNTRY FOR MARLYS ANY MORE.

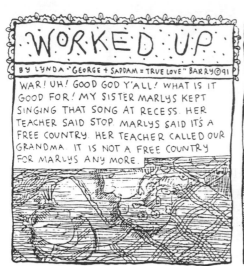

OR ME. OUR GRANDMA SAID MARLYS WOULDN'T BE SO WORKED UP ABOUT THE WAR IF IT WASN'T FOR ME. WE GOT A NEW RULE AT OUR HOUSE. NO TALKING ABOUT IT. IF IT COMES ON THE TV, TURN IT OFF. IF YOU WANT TO TALK ABOUT WAR THEN GO OVER TO MR. LUDERMYER'S WHO SAYS JUST BOMB THEM ALL AND LET GOD SORT THEM OUT LATER

LAST NIGHT MARLYS WOKE ME UP TO SAY HER DREAM. IT WAS THAT ALL THE PEOPLE WHO GOT BOMBED WENT INTO THE MATTRESS OF THE PRESIDENT. SHE SAID HIS BED WAS VERY HIGH. I THINK THE DREAM WAS FROM THAT STORY "THE PRINCESS AND THE PEA". DIFFERENCE WAS THOUGH, THE PRESIDENT COULD SLEEP.

MY GRANDMA SAYS THERES NOT A DAMN THING I CAN DO ABOUT THE WAR. BUT SHE IS WRONG. I CAN YELL STOP. I CAN SHOUT IT AND SAY IT AND WRITE IT AND THINK IT. I WANT TO BE THE EVIDENCE THAT NOT EVERYONE HERE SAID IT'S OK TO KILL THE PEOPLE THERE. NOT EVERYONE HERE THINKS AMERICANS COUNT MORE TO GOD. IN MY BEDROOM MY PRAYER IS SILENT NIGHT NO BOMBS. HOLY NIGHT NO KILLING. ALL IS CALM PEACE.

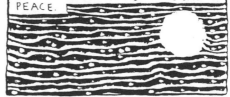

Lynda Barry

Roz Chast

—Housework Avoidance—

Alice Muhlback

Haphazard Housekeeper

Eons of earth
Shield artifacts
Of citizens and kings;
Dust is my preservative,
Protectin all my things.

I make no apology:
I'm aiding archeology.

Annie Komorny

Housewives in Hell

Anne Gibbons

Nicole Hollander

Gall Machlis

Housecleaning

i always liked housecleaning
even as a child
i dug straightening
the cabinets
putting new paper on
the shelves
washing the refrigerator
inside out
and unfortunately this habit has
carried over and i find
i must remove you
from my life

Nikki Giovanni

Dianne Reum

Anne Gibbons

Anne Gibbons

OVER COFFEE

© JACKIE URBANOVIC 1985 #2

REMEMBER WHEN YOU WERE YOUNG, AND ALL YOU DREAMED OF WAS BEING TAKEN CARE OF BY SOMEONE WONDERFUL LIKE VALENTINO?....

Yes.

CAB CALLOWAY... WHAT!

WELL, IT'S NOT ALL IT'S MADE UP TO BE!!

POP

WHAT?!

DON'T GO MESSIN' WITH MY DREAMS AT THIS LATE DATE, GIRL!

GIRL, WHATTA YOU MEAN TELLING ME PRINCE CHARMING IS DEAD?

WELL, WHEN I WAS YOUNG I HAD LOTS OF KIDS, WORK, AND DEBT...

SO?

BUT NOW THE KIDS ARE GONE AND WE'RE WELL OFF.

SO?

SO JOE KEEPS TRYING TO MAKE MY LIFE EASY.

SO, HE BOUGHT ME A CUISINART, A NO-WAX FLOOR, AND EVEN A MAID! EVERYTHING IS TAKEN CARE OF,

HE'S BECOME A REAL PRINCE CHARMING!

SO?!

SO I DON'T WANT A **PRINCE!!**

I WANT A FLOOR TO WASH!!

SO?!

OH.

Jackie Urbanovic

Judy Horacek

GEORGE

Mary Lawton

Kate Gawf

appliances

Jennifer Camper

Injustice

Though complex modern sciences
Explore space with dexterity.
My simple home appliances
Fail with regularity.

American technology
Owes me an apology.

Annie Komorny

No Machine

The day phone machines were invented, I bought one.
It was always on, but not everyone was used to them yet.
One day I left it turned off by mistake.
A friend called.
"No machine...How strange."
She was certain something was terribly wrong.
Margaret called the phone company and complained,
"I called Flash, but all the phone did was ring and ring and ring."
The repair department wearily offered,
"Maybe she's not home."

Flash Rosenberg

GET-WELL CARDS
for
UNDER-THE-WEATHER APPLIANCES

GET WELL
SOON!

Contrast's gone?
Picture shot?
Don't know what it is
you've got?
You'll soon be fixed,
but even so
We miss your cheerful
little glow.

IN THE
SHOP?

Cold blows warm,
Hot blows cold
Fact is, friend,
you're getting old.
HOPE YOU'RE
REPAIRED SOON

TO A SICK
DRYER...

You burned a shirt,
You charred the socks,
You gave the folks electric
shocks.
A leaky hose, a missing screw,
We hope that's all that's
wrong with you.

Roz Chast

The "Flash Time O-Dometer"

I love those catalogs of electronic gadgets.
However, one essential device is missing.
Given the state of marital bickering
the world desperately needs a "Flash Time-O-Dometer".
This Marriage-Saving device accurately measures
the time each person waits for the other person.
A running account issuing time credits & debits is digitally tallied.
No more inexact arguments over who was late, again.
Contrary to popular misconception, women wait far more often than men.
In test markets, Mrs. Cracker discovered she had earned 11 years credit
while waiting for her husband over the course of a 38 year marriage.
Why in just three years, Mrs. Woodrow has earned a year and a half.
This time is credited to the end of your life
if unredeemable during the couple's time together.
This is the real reason why women live longer than men.

Flash Rosenberg

Martha Campbell

THEY'RE TOUGH!
THEY'RE ENIGMATIC!
THEY'VE MYSTIFIED
US ALL SINCE
CHILDHOOD!
SURE, YOU MIGHT
JOG OR **WORK
OUT** A LITTLE, BUT

...ARE YOU A
**REAL
JOCK?**
ANOTHER ILLUMINATING QUIZ
by MISS DELILAH B. SCONE

AS A CHILD, YOUR FAVORITE GAME WAS:
a.) DODGE BALL   c.) HOUSE
b.) KICK THE CAN   d.) OLD MAID

HOW'S YOUR **ENDURANCE?**
AFTER A BRISK
5-MILE JOG, YOU
FEEL:
a.) WARMED-UP AND
    READY TO GO
b.) SELF-SATISFIED
c.) LIKE YOU'RE GOING
    TO BE SICK
d.) SICK

WHEN YOU SEE AN EMPTY
BEER CAN, YOU ARE
COMPELLED TO:
a.) CRUSH IT WITH
    ONE HAND
b.) CRUSH IT WITH
    WHATEVER IT TAKES
c.) REDEEM IT
d.) USE IT FOR AN
    ASHTRAY

YOUR FAVORITE POSITION IN SOFTBALL IS:
a.) SHORTSTOP   c.) RIGHT FIELD
b.) LEFT FIELD   d.) ON THE BENCH

IF SOMEONE GAVE YOU A MEMBERSHIP TO THE
LOCAL 'Y', YOU WOULD IMMEDIATELY SIGN
UP FOR CLASSES IN:
a.) POWERLIFTING   c.) AEROBICS
b.) SELF-DEFENSE   d.) MEDITATION

YOUR SPORTS FANTASY
IS TO:
a.) PLAY IN THE SUPER
    BOWL
b.) FINISH A MARATHON
c.) GET A GRAND SLAM
    IN BRIDGE
d.) COLLECT $100 OFF
    YOUR $10 SUPER
    BOWL BET

SCORE YOURSELF:
FOR EVERY 'A' ANSWER, SCORE 3 POINTS
B = 2 POINTS,   C = 1 POINT, D = 0 POINTS.
what you are:
0-5 = AN UNREPENTANT COUCH POTATO
6-10 = A WIMP
11-14 = A NOUVEAU ATHLETE
15-18 = OUCH! YOU WIN! YES, YOU'RE A
REAL JOCK!

Alison Bechdel

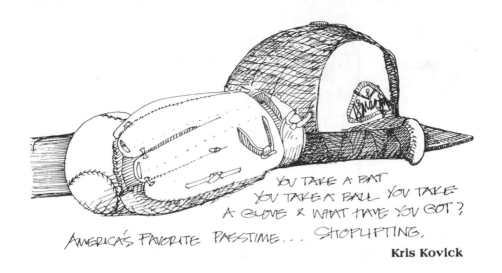

YOU TAKE A BAT
YOU TAKE A BALL YOU TAKE
A GLOVE & WHAT HAVE YOU GOT?
AMERICA'S FAVORITE PASSTIME... SHOPLIFTING.

Kris Kovick

The Couch Potato

Deep in the pillows he snuggles. A lump
My dedicated sofa chump.

Turn on the set. Start up the game.
Whatever the sport — it's all the same.

A ball of any size or speed,
Any Lendl, any Snead.

Let them kick it or sink it or dunk it or whack it,
Go at it with bat or club or racket,

There he lies, my chubby hubby,
Tracking every Met and Cubbie,

With a good supply of beer and chips
For slow-motion bites and languid sips,

Now and then he announces the score.
Of life at home he asks no more.

I pat him in passing and tell myself this,
One of us two has found perfect bliss.

Vesle Fenstermaker

Nicole Hollander

"When I realized I wasn't doing it for him anymore... I began to enjoy it..."

Stephanie Piro

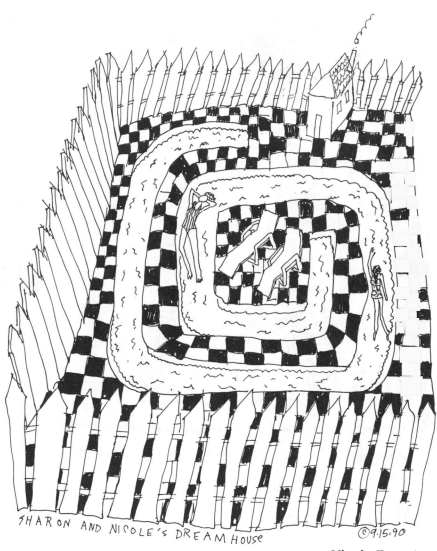

SHARON AND NICOLE'S DREAM HOUSE   ©9.15.90

Nicole Ferentz

Faking It

(A Woman confides in the audience while a Man in an easy chair watches a football game.)

WOMAN: This is really embarrassing—but I've gotta tell somebody.
MAN: *(pointing to the set)* Oh, look at this, babe!
(She goes over, sits on the arm of his chair, and watches.)
MAN: Now they've got the ball on the thirty-yard line.
WOMAN: *(getting into it)* Ohh, that's great.
MAN: First down.
WOMAN: Mmm—yes.
MAN: They got plenty of time—he oughta try a pass.
WOMAN: Instead of handing it off—oh, that's good, yes.
MAN: Yeah. He's got the receivers, for Christ's sake.
WOMAN: Oh, God, yes.
MAN: Okay, here we go—
(The Woman moans. The play happens.)
MAN: He's out of the pocket, he's gonna throw—
WOMAN: *(aroused)* Throw it, throw it!
MAN: Martin's got it on the ten!
WOMAN: Oh, God, yes!
MAN: The five!
WOMAN: YES!
MAN: Touchdown!
WOMAN: *(orgasmic)* AAAH!
(They both settle down again, and he lights two cigarettes.)
MAN: *(handing her a cigarette)* Great stuff, huh?
WOMAN: The best, honey.
(The Woman comes back over to the audience.)
WOMAN: I just—*(tosses the cigarette on the floor and stomps it)*—I can't keep this secret any longer. *(after a pause)* He thinks I'm enjoying the game, but—I'm faking it. It's not that there's anything wrong with me. I just can't seem to get excited the way he does. If we could rent a good movie, something with real relationships and emotions, it would be different. But he doesn't like that sort of thing. I can't even get him to try it.
MAN: Hey—they got the extra point.
WOMAN: *(to Man)* Ooh—fantastic. *(back to the audience)* So—this is it. Sometimes I think of telling him, confessing everything—but I'm afraid if he knew he'd be hurt. And he'd think I'd been faking it every single time, when there was that one Super Bowl.... *(sighing)* Oh, I don't

know. It's not really fair to me or him, but I guess for now I'll just have to watch movies that satisfy me when he's out, and I'm alone. It's a compromise, but—what can I say? *(shrugs)* At least our sex life's good.

MAN: *(announcing)* Kick-off!

(The Woman goes back and settles herself on the arm of the chair again.)

MAN: *(watching the action)* Okay—Fryar's bringing it out to the twenty—

WOMAN: More—

MAN: The twenty-five—

WOMAN: MORE—

MAN: The thirty—

WOMAN: YES—

MAN: The thirty-five—

WOMAN: OH, DON'T STOP!

Blackout

Julia Willis

Barbara Brandon

religion & philosophy

Nina Paley

I Think Therefore I Must Have A Snack

A popular misconception is that all the most famous philosophers were old white guys who lived in ivory towers out of touch with real folks. Well, they were. But in addition to their preoccupation with discerning the meaning of life, they also worried about things like whether their socks matched and if they should pay the cost of their dates' babysitters. For example:

Friedrich Nietzsche

Friedrich Nietzsche's famous quote: "What does not kill you makes you stronger," was simply a little ditty he worked up for his health club t-shirt. This is the same health club where he worked on his concepts of "super-man" and the "will to power" which had a major impact on the development of bicep curls and tricep extensions.

Soren Kierkegaard

Danish philosopher Soren Kierkegaard — a forerunner to the existentialists—also made a practical discovery which changed the course of civilization. Colleagues at international philosophy conferences began calling him "Whiz" Kierkegaard after he injected a cheese-like substance into aerosol cans, creating the first artificial party food.

Martin Heidegger

Though German philosopher Martin Heidegger criticized modern technology, he played a major role in the development of aluminum siding, deoderizing insoles, and the poodle skirt. He felt his greatest failures were making up the rules that redheads should not wear pink and that blue and green did not go together. Both propositions were disproved in the sixties.

Jean-Paul Sarte

Jean-Paul Sartre enraged the French perfume industry with his vision of man as master of his own fate when he stated: "Existence preceeds essence." Perfume sales plummeted as buyers pondered whether there was any point in smelling good if man is indefinable. Others argued that it might be easier to find him in the dark. Until Sartre, the principle foundation for all knowledge and reality in the perfume industry was Descartes' proposition: "I smell, therefore I am."

Plato

Around 400 B.C. Plato attacked hedonism and the concept of "might is right." This got him thrown out of his college fraternity for being no fun at parties and football games, even though he is credited with organizing the first toga party.

Georg Wilhelm Friedrich Hegel

German philosopher Hegel's dialectical method —a big hit because it did not require batteries —involved challenging a thesis with an antithesis and reconciling them in a synthesis. The process of synthesis led to the creation of polyester/cotton blends which were a great boon to the underwear industry.

Pat Miller

ENTREE PHILOSOPHER

Terry Harned

HOLY MAYO

Mary Lawton

Flash Rosenberg

Are You Jewish? Take This Test & Find Out

1. There are no Jews living in
    a. sin
    b. El Paso
    c. trailer parks

2. The cleaning lady in a Jewish household is expected to
    a. do windows
    b. make latkes
    c. attend all bar mitzvahs and weddings

3. To make a good pet for a Jewish child, an animal must be
    a. gentle
    b. housebroken
    c. stuffed

4. Jews spend their vacations
    a. sightseeing
    b. sunbathing
    c. discussing where they spent their last vacation and where they'll spend the next

5. A Jewish mouth never
    a. lies
    b. closes
    c. contains gold teeth

6. If there's a hairdresser in your immediate family, you are
    a. up on the newest styles
    b. entitled to free haircuts
    c. not Jewish

7. Wilderness means
    a. no running water
    b. no electricity
    c. no hot-and-sour soup

8. The most popular outdoor sport among Jews is
    a. jogging
    b. tennis
    c. howling over the neighbors' lawn ornaments

9. Jews never drive
    a. unsafely
    b. on Saturdays
    c. eighteen-wheelers

10. A truly unsuitable gift for a Jewish person is
    a. Easter lilies
    b. a crucifix
    c. a Zippo lighter

11. A Jewish skydiver is
    a. careful
    b. insured
    c. an apparition

12. Jews never eat at restaurants that
    a. aren't kosher
    b. cost too much
    c. have paintings for sale

13. No Jewish person in history has ever been known to
    a. become a prostitute
    b. deface a synagogue
    c. remove the back of a TV set

14. There is no such thing as a Jewish
    a. black belt
    b. obscene caller
    c. toll collector

15. Jews never sing
    a. off-key
    b. "Nel Blu di Pinto di Blu"
    c. around a piano bar

16. You won't catch a Jewish person on a
    a. horse
    b. backhoe
    c. toot

17. Jews are ambivalent about
    a. vegetarianism
    b. Jesse Jackson
    c. absolutely nothing

SCORING: Take 1 point for each *a* answer, 2 for each *b*, 3 for
      each *c.*

Molly Katz
excerpt from *Jewish as a Second Language*

Jackie Urbanovic

The Pope Says...

Arja Kajermo

Confession

We were Catholic so we went to confession a lot. I wasn't a very bad child and I could never think of anything really significant to confess. The nuns at school said that anyone who had the audacity to think that they could go a day in their lives without sinning was pretty arrogant and would be in deep caca on judgment day. So naturally I felt terrible about not being able to think of any decent sins. So I made up things. Which means I lied. Which was a sin. For which I then felt guilty

Not only that, it seemed to be the one sin which couldn't be erased by going to confession. I mean, I wasn't about to go to confession and confess that I'd lied in confession. The nuns said you could confess absolutely anything and the priest would never tell. But I knew better. I knew for a fact that if the sin were bad enough, that priest would run right over and tell my mother everything.

So I had this permanent black spot on my soul. There it sat, while other, smaller black spots appeared and disappeared as I went in and out of the confessional box—and I just had to hope I didn't get run over by a truck, because if you die with one of those big ones on there, it's doomsday.

Kate Gawf

excerpt from *The Incredible Embarrassment of Being*

Flash Rosenberg

Judy Horacek

Original Sin

My mother (who is a sweet Southern Methodist lady) taught me quite early about original sin: "Well, one time," she would say, "Eve had this apple, and she took a bite of it, and she thought it was pretty good, so naturally she wanted to share it with everybody. So when she saw Adam, she gave it to him to let him have some. He took one bite, and then another, and another, and then his eyes lit up and he said, 'Damn, woman—I got me a great idea. If we can get a whole bunch of these things, and keep 'em hid, stick 'em in the cellar or freeze dry 'em or something, hold 'em off the market till there's nothing to eat around here and the price goes sky high and all our children are starving—why, honey, we'll make a fuckin' fortune!' Now that, darlin'," my Mama'd finish, "is what you call Original Sin."

Julia Willis

Q: How can you explain human suffering if there is a God?
A: Shouldn't God be the one explaining?

Patricia Marx

We Are All One

Dear Tofu Roshi:

Another dreaded Saturday night has rolled around again, I don't have a date, and I'm sitting at home alone feeling sorry for myself, driven deep into the New York Super Fudge Chunk ice cream by my terrible sense of isolation. But I recently heard that our suffering is caused by the illusion of the separate self, and that in truth we are all one. Does this mean that really I am spending the evening at a vegetarian restaurant with a strong but sensitive fiance, planning our Buddhist wedding in a northern California temple garden and our subsequent honeymoon trekking in the Himalayas?

Wallflower

Dear Wallflower

We are all one. We are all already enlightened, if only we knew it. And by the same token, as you suggest, you are already married and trekking in the Himalayas, and you're getting a blister, but your husband forgot the moleskin. As your understanding penetrates still deeper, you realize that you have already grown weary of each other's foibles, and you are already divorced. It's Saturday night, and you're enjoying a quiet evening at home — writing a letter to me, and savoring a favorite taste treat.

Tofu Roshi

Susan Moon

The God

I have no use
for Zeus.
He'd slay
to get his way
and change his shape
to rape
and I'm sure any error
he'd blame on Hera.

Lillian Morrison

Preacher Don't Send Me

Preacher, don't send me
when I die
to some big ghetto
in the sky
where rats eat cats
of the leopard type
and Sunday brunch
is grits and tripe.

I've known those rats
I've seen them kill
and grits I've had
would make a hill,
or maybe a mountain,
so what I need
from you on Sunday
is a different creed.

Preacher, please don't
promise me
streets of gold
and milk for free.
I stopped all milk
at four years old
and once I'm dead
I won't need gold.

I'd call a place
pure paradise

where families are loyal
and strangers are nice,
where the music is jazz
and the season is fall.
Promise me that
or nothing at all.

Maya Angelou

vacation

Rina Piccolo

My Favorite Vacation

When people ask me where I'm going on my vacation, I look them squarely in the eye and answer "the bathroom."

No one ever bothers you when you're in the bathroom. And what goes on behind that door is rarely discussed. Quite honestly, no one wants to know what you do in the bathroom. Each person has their own memories of time spent alone in that space, but they aren't the kind of stories that you share around a campfire.

When we were youngsters, bathrooming was a tag team sport. We'd go in pairs and compare style and statistics. There were no inhibitions. We were young, and curious, and we had to go. But as we grew older and social graces were learned, we became aware that we could not go together to a place where there was only one seat.

As adults, we address the whole subject of bathrooms in a very businesslike manner. Most people think it's a great place to wallpaper, but they wouldn't want to live there. Personally, I keep a pillow and a favorite book stashed in the back of the linen closet. Whenever things get too tense or I just feel like getting away from it all for a few minutes, I lock the door, stretch out in the tub, (dry), and read a couple of chapters. No ringing telephones or blaring televisions, no pets or kids to contend with; just peace and solitude. Privacy in the bathroom is an unwritten law that transcends all cultures. Even a Jehovah's Witness will turn away from your door if told that you're "indisposed."

Perhaps bathroom is just a state of mind. When your boss is yelling at you, red-lining the report that you spent days preparing and you just can't take it anymore, just close your eyes and repeat to yourself softly, "I'm in the bathroom. I'm in the bathroom." Not only will you meditate yourself into a harmonious tranquility, I'll bet that your boss drops the subject and gives you the rest of the day off.

Sometimes at night I'll fill the tub, dim the lights and listen to the crickets chirping outside the window while I gaze at the still water and become one with nature. Why pack a camper and drive hours in heavy traffic to get away from it all? True sanctuary can be found up the stairs, second door on the left.

Want to see the vacation photos. . . ?

Penny Lorio

Vacation Plans

We won't need a fancy trailer, Dear,
Nor all of the latest camping gear.
My needs are simple, my wants are few—
Just any old plushy motel will do.

Annie Komorny

Judy Horacek

The Wander Woman's Phrase Book

On the Street

Good day.
Bonjour.

Good afternoon.
Bonjour.

Good evening.
Bonsoir.

Same to you.
Vous aussi.

I'm not interested.
Ça ne m'intéresse pas.

In that either.
Cela non plus.

Stop following me.
Arrêtez de me suivre.

I wish to be alone.
Je voudrais être seule.

I am trying to think.
Je suis en train de réfléchir.
To read.　　　　　　　　　　　*de lire.*

I am trying to sleep.
Je veux dormir.

I prefer my own company, if you don't mind.
Je préfère être seule, si ca vous fait rien.

Please do not disturb me.
Ne me dérangez pas!

I have an extremely contagious disease.
Je souffre d'une maladie extrêmement contagieuse.

You are an insult to your country.
Vous faites honte à votre pays.

City	*ville*
Village	*village*
Mother.	*mere.*

Get away.
Fichez le camp!

Leave me alone, you animal.
Fichez-moi la paix, espèce de mufle.

Pig	*de cochon*
Imbecile.	*d'imbécile.*

Please.
S'il vous plait.

If you don't stop.
Si vous n'arrêtez pas

Move	*ne bougez pas*
Behave like a gentleman.	*n'agissez pas en homme bien élevé.*

I'll call the police.
J'appellerai la police.

Help!
Au secours!

Police!
Police!

I hope I didn't hurt you too badly.
J'espere ne vous avoir pas trop de mal.

Excuse me.
Pardon.

Alison Owings

deep in the heart of TEXAS

a wild 'n' wooly graphic story by NINA PALEY ©'91

116

Nina Paley

117

Too Wussy for Texas

Biggest fight we've had all summer here in the Great State is over what motto to put on our license plates. The Highway Commission voted early this summer to put *Texas—The Friendship State* on our plates. This was unanimously condemned as Too Wussy for Texas, and it took Bubba a couple of months to get it turned around.

Historians will recall that we had the same flap a few years ago when some unusually demented Highway Commissioners decided *Texas—The Wildflower State* would look good on our plates. This caused the ever-vigilant guardians of Texas *machismo* to declare that we might as well call it *The Gay Rights State.*

Now, *The Friendship State* is not nearly as wussy a motto as *The Wildflower State*—and it does have cultural roots. Our state motto is *Friendship,* and our state safety slogan is *Drive Friendly,* which is ungrammatical but perfectly clear.

And it wouldn't be false advertising—Texans actually are friendlier than normal people—at least outside big cities, which you can prove any day by driving into a Texas town and saying "Hidy."

But we do have a shitkicker image to maintain, so the papers have been rife with suggestions like *Yankee Go Home,* and *Fuck Alaska,* and *Texas: Kiss My Ass.*

If we were to go for honesty instead of public relations, we'd wind up with something like *Too Much Is not Enough* or *Texas—Land of Wretched Excess.* Or, perhaps, *Home of the FDIC.*

If honesty were a national license plate policy, we'd see:

- *Rhode Island—Land of Obscurity*
- *Oklahoma—The Recruiting Violations State*
- *Maine—Home of George Bush*
- *Minnesota—Too Damn Cold*
- *Wisconsin—Eat Cheese or Die*
- *California—Freeway Congestion with Occassional Gunfire*
- *New Jersey—Armpit of the Nation*
- *North Dakota—Incredibly Boring*
- *Nebraska—More Interesting Than North Dakota*
- *New York—We're Not Arrogant, We're Just Better Than You*

It was a slow summer for scandal here until Bo Pilgrim, an East Texas chicken magnate, walked onto the floor of the State Senate and started handing out $10,000 checks with no payee filled in. He said he wanted to encourage the senators, then meeting in special session on the workers' compensation issue, to do right by bidness.

Turns out it's perfectly legal to walk onto the Senate floor and start handing out checks for $10,000 made out to no one in particular. Just another campaign contribution, folks. Bo Pilgrim is a familiar sight on Texas television, where he dresses up in a pilgrim suit and pitches ads for his fowl. He adds a certain *je ne sais quoi* to our communal life. His chicken factory is a major source of pollution in East Texas so, of course, the governor put him on the state Water Quality Board.

The death of Houston congressman Mickey Leland made so many hearts ache that poor Mick like to got buried under a mountain of hagiography. But you can't make a saint of a guy who laughed as much as Mickey.

My favorite Leland stories go back to the early 1970s, when he came to the Texas Legislature, one of the first blacks ever elected right out of a black district without having to get white folks' permission to run at-large. He showed up wearing an Afro and dashikis, and the Bubbas thought he was some kind of freak-radical Black Panther, and it meant the end of the world was at hand.

His first session Leland carried a generic-drug bill to help poor, sick, old people. He couldn't believe anyone would vote against poor, sick, old folks, but the drug companies and the doctors teamed up to beat his bill. After the vote, he stalked up to the medical-association lobbyists at the back of the House and in a low voice that shook with fury he hissed, "You are evil motherfuckers." They almost wet their pants on the spot. He got the bill passed in the next session.

During the 1975 speaker's race, members of the Black Caucus made a shrewd political play—they deserted the liberal-labor candidate and threw their support to Billy Wayne Clayton, a West Texas redneck, in exchange for some major committee chairmanships and heavy clout. Leland came out of the meeting with Clayton waving a tiny Confederate flag and announced, "We done sold de plantation."

I remember wondering early on if guys like Mickey were going to make a difference in the Lege. One day during his first session I saw him standing in the middle of the capitol rotunda, which is a natural amplifier, trying to get Craig Washington and Paul Ragsdale, who were peering down at him from the third-floor gallery, to come along. In a voice that stopped traffic he yelled up, "Gottdammit, are you niggers comin' down to get lunch, or what?" Yep, gonna make a difference.

And he did. He made a much bigger difference in this world than all the damned old racists who used to vote against him.

Molly Ivins

Crisis addict

gasp!

Mary Lawton

They're Getting Ahead of You

One day in late 1969, in the research library of the University of California at Berkeley, a young man went berserk. He ran through the library, shouting hysterically at his astonished fellow students, "Stop! Stop! You're getting ahead of me!"

He was arrested. But what was his crime, really? *Being in the wrong decade.* As we all know, the sixties era, and its childish preoccupation with peace, good sex, and battered VW buses, was little more than a black mark, a shameful demerit in the History of Stress.

Now, of course, in the stress-filled eighties, this concept of "getting ahead of me" has regained its rightful place of importance. In fact, it is one of the basic precepts of stress.

Simply stated, *people are getting ahead of you.* All the time.

While you're at your desk, people working out at the gym are getting ahead of you.

While you're at the gym, your co-workers are getting ahead of you.

If a friend gets a promotion at work, she has gotten ahead of you.

If a colleague reads a book you haven't read, he has gotten ahead of you.

The entire U.S. swim team has gotten ahead of you.

While you're reading this book, *everyone* is getting ahead of you.

The beauty of this concept is that it can be applied across the board, anywhere, anytime.

On the road? Drivers of more expensive cars have gotten ahead of you.

Watching TV? All the writers, actors, and technical crews have gotten ahead of you.

At Marine World? The *dolphins* have gotten ahead of you.

Always judge yourself, and your intrinsic moral worth, in terms of specific achievements as compared to others.

Always judge any situation in relation to how much the people involved have gotten ahead of you, and in what ways.

Pamela Pettler
excerpt from *The Joy of Stress*

Marian Henley

SYLVIA

Nicole Hollander

"Magnum"

He was gone. But she didn't need him. She didn't need a Man to feel safe... living in the city. What she needed was, maybe, a .357 Magnum...

Stephanie Piro

Annie Lawson

124

She lived in the state of fear.

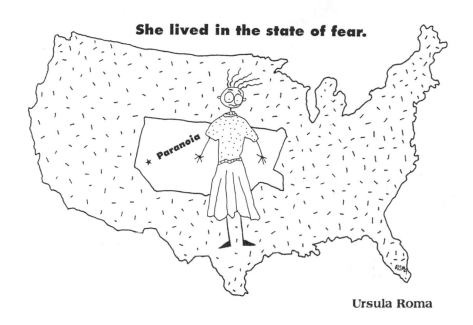

Ursula Roma

Lynda Barry

FROM THE TOURNAMENT OF NEUROSES PARADE

The "I Never Really Broke Away From My Parents" Float

The "In My Mind's Eye, I Will Always Be a Fat, Short, Frizzy-Haired, Glasses-and-Braces-Wearing Sixth Grader" Float

The "People Who Have Difficulty Forming Bonds of Intimacy with Other People" Float

The "I Only Want What Is Unattainable" Float

The "Hypochondria" Float

The "Fear of Chickens" Float

Roz Chast

poultry

After Mike walked out, she decided to give up Men and raise chickens. Chickens didn't stay out all night, or come home drunk, or sleep with your best girlfriend...

And if they did... you could cut off their heads and eat them...

Stephanie Piro

© 1980 T.O. SYLVESTER

"Don't look now, but I think Helen is planning another escape."

T.O. Sylvester

CHICK'N-in-a-THIMBLE
THE RESTAURANT FOR PEOPLE WHO EAT LIKE BIRDS!

1/4 chicken	$3.95		1/256 chicken	$.29
1/8 chicken	$2.49		1/512 chicken	$.19
1/16 chicken	$1.49		1/1,024 chicken	$.13
1/32 chicken	$.99		1/2,048 chicken	$.09
1/64 chicken	$.59		1/4,096 chicken	$.06
1/128 chicken	$.39		1/8,192 chicken	$.04

Roz Chast

"HENRIETTA'S RASH WAS WORSE THAN WE THOUGHT. IT WAS PAPRIKA."

Martha Campbell

Menu

We got crispy chicken
we got frisky chicken
we got digital chicken
we got Chicken Evergreen

We got chicken salad
we got chicken with rice
we got radar chicken
we got chicken in the first degree

but we ain't got no fried chicken.

We got Chicken Red Light
we got drive-in chicken
we got felony chicken
we got chicken gravy

but we ain't got no fried chicken.

We got half a chicken
we got 2 chickens
we got Chicken Tylenol
we got chicken on ice

but we ain't got no fried chicken.

We got King Chicken
we got chicken a la mode
we got no-lead chicken

We got chainsaw chicken
we got chicken in a chair
we got borderline chicken
we got Chicken for the Young at Heart

We got aerosol chicken
we got Chicken Guitar

but we ain't got no fried chicken.

We got Coast Guard Chicken
we got sixpack chicken
we got Chicken Las Vegas
we got chicken to burn

but we ain't got no fried chicken.

We got 10-speed chicken
we got atomic chicken
we got chicken on tape

We got day-care chicken
we got Chicken Mascara
we got second-hand chicken

but we ain't got no fried chicken.

We got dead chicken
we got chicken on the hoof
we got open admissions chicken
we got Chicken Motel

We got astronaut chicken
we got chicken to go

We got gospel chicken
we got four-wheel drive chicken
we got chain gang chicken
we got chicken transfusions

but we ain't got no fried chicken

We got wrong turn chicken
we got rough draft chicken
we got chicken sodas
we got Chicken Deluxe

but we ain't
got
no

fried chicken.
                    June Jordan & Sara Miles

Jennifer Berman

Rina Piccolo

Theresa Henry Smith

Pointers for Pets

I feel compelled by duty to begin this discourse with what I actually think of as a statement, but what will more probably be construed as an admission. I do not like animals. Of any sort. I don't even like the idea of animals. Animals are no friends of mine. They are not welcome in my house. They occupy no space in my heart. Animals are off my list. I will say, however, in the spirit of qualification, that I mean them no particular harm. I won't bother animals if animals won't bother me. Well, perhaps I had better amend that last sentence. I won't personally bother animals. I do feel, though, that a plate bereft of a good cut of something rare is an affront to the serious diner, and that while I have frequently run across the fellow who could, indeed, be described as a broccoli-and-potatoes man, I cannot say that I have ever really taken to such a person.

Therefore, I might more accurately state that I do not like animals, with two exceptions. The first being in the past tense, at which point I like them just fine, in the form of nice crispy spareribs and Bass Weejun penny loafers. And the second being outside, by which I mean not merely outside, as in outside the house, but genuinely outside, as in outside in the woods, or preferably outside in the South American jungle. This is, after all, only fair. I don't go there; why should they come here?

The above being the case, it should then come as no surprise that I do not approve of the practice of keeping animals as pets. "Not approve" is too mild: pets should be disallowed by law. Especially dogs. Especially in New York City.

I have not infrequently verbalized this sentiment in what now passes for polite society, and have invariably been the recipient of the information that even if dogs should be withheld from the frivolous, there would still be the blind and the pathologically lonely to think of. I am not totally devoid of compassion, and after much thought I believe that I have hit upon the perfect solution to this problem: let the lonely lead the blind. The implementation of this plan would provide companionship to one and a sense of direction to the other, without inflicting on the rest of the populace the all too common spectacle of grown men addressing german shepherds in the respectful tones best reserved for elderly clergymen and Internal Revenue agents.

You animal lovers uninterested in helping news dealers across busy intersections will just have to seek companionship elsewhere. If actual friends are not within your grasp, may I suggest that you take a cue from your favorite celebrity and consider investing in a really good entourage. The advantages of such a scheme are inestimable: an entourage is indisputably superior to a dog (or even, of course, actual friends), and will begin to pay for itself almost immediately. You do not have to walk an entourage; on the contrary, one of the major functions of an entourage is that it walks you. You do not have to name an entourage. You do not have to play with an entourage. You do not have to take an entourage to the vet—although the conscientious entourage owner makes certain that his entourage has had all of its shots. You do, of course, have to feed an entourage, but this can be accomplished in decent Italian restaurants and without the bother and mess of large tin cans and special plastic dishes.

If the entourage suggestion does not appeal to you, perhaps you should alter your concept of companionship. Living things need not enter into it at all. Georgian silver and Duncan Phyfe sofas make wonderful companions, as do all alcoholic beverages and out-of-season fruits. Use your imagination, study up on the subject. You'll think of something.

If, however, you do not think of something—and animal lovers being a singularly intractable lot, chances are that you won't—I have decided to direct the remainder of my remarks to the pets themselves with dignity and grace.

- If you are a dog and your owner suggests that you wear a sweater ... suggest that he wear a tail.

- If you have been named after a human being of artistic note, run away from home. It is unthinkable that even an animal should be obliged to share quarters with anyone who calls a cat Ford Madox Ford.

- Dogs who earn their living by appearing in television commercials in which they constantly and aggressively demand meat should remember that in at least one Far Eastern country they *are* meat.

• If you are only a bird in a gilded cage—count your blessings.

• A dog who thinks he is man's best friend is a dog who obviously has never met a tax lawyer.

• If you are an owl being kept as a pet, I applaud and encourage your tendency to hoot. You are to be highly commended for expressing such a sentiment. An owl is, of course, not a pet at all; it is an unforgivable and wistful effort in the direction of whimsy.

• No animal should ever jump up on the dining-room furniture unless absolutely certain that he can hold his own in the conversation.

Fran Lebowitz

FOR ONE WILD MOMENT,
HAVING LEFT THE TURTLEBOWL,
ARIEL FELT ALMOST FREE!

AAAHHHGGG!

Roz Warren

Move Over, Uri Geller!

He stares at the door
And his molecules buzz
And will it to open
And lo! It does!
Unblinking, he stares
At his empty dish
And presto! It's filled
With his favorite fish!
My cat has a power
At his command
To psychokinetically
Move my hand.

Dorothy Heller

Ode to a Siamese without a Uterus

She doesn't yowl as darkness falls,
She doesn't look for things with balls.

She doesn't scratch the furniture,
She pads around, oh so mature.

I don't call her a pussy cat:
She's really only half of that!

Sally Grab

SYLVIA

Nicole Hollander

Rina Piccolo

Lee Binswanger

food

Kate Gawf

BEAUTY AND HEALTH

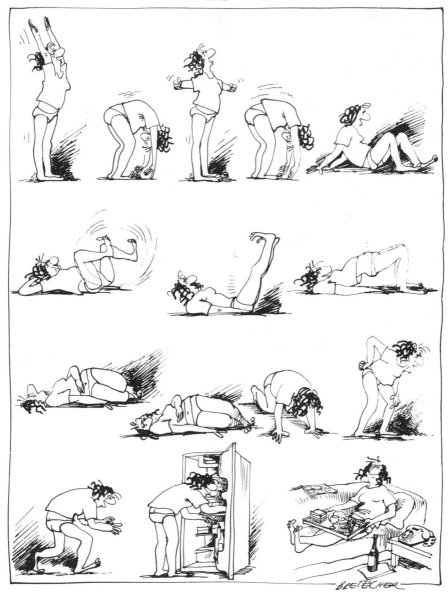

Claire Bretecher

Gravy

No religion, no politics, no sex at the supper table. Mother does the cooking. Mother makes the rules.

Mother cooks stew, calls it vegetarian stew even though it has chunks of beef in it. I eat Mother's stew even though I call myself a vegetarian. Mother assures me that the meat she buys is so lean that there's not a chance in hell that one fat globule could melt into the gravy. I don't tell her it's blood, not fat, that alarms me. She picks out the meat with plastic pickle tongs that she got free at a tupperware party, before passing me a plateful. She discards my meat on Father's plate.

"Who ever heard of broccoli in stew?" Father says, picking out the little green trees and piling them on my plate. I eat the top off a tiny one, after smelling it. I want to ask my parents if they think the broccoli smells like meat but I'm afraid that might lead to breaking Mother's rules.

I get pumpernickle bread out of the freezer and nuke it in the microwave for thirty seconds so we can sop up the nonfat gravy. When I sit back down Mother is trading green beans for pearl onions with Father.

"Anybody want to trade gravy?" I ask. "No thank you," Father says. "I don't eat vegetarian gravy."

"This isn't vegetarian gravy, it's brown," I say.

"Alright, I don't eat a vegetarians' gravy," Father says.

Mother says "Vegetarian gravy can be brown. You just add a little worstershire and a little gravymaster."

Father takes a spoonful of gravy from my bowl, tastes it, shakes his head, says, "No protein. You got unnatural gravy."

I take the spoon out of his hand and have a taste of his gravy. "Hormones" I say. "Antibiotics. Pesticides."

We must be talking about religion, politics, or sex, because Mother takes her plate into the den.

I follow her. "Ma, do you like the smell of broccoli?" I ask, contrite, by way of polite conversation.

"Ask me after I finish my meal," she says.

Father comes in with a second plate of meat laden-stew.

Mother gives us both a warning glance. "Put on 'Wheel of Fortune'," she says.

Father and I sit on the couch, on opposite sides of Mother. We finish our stew and watch Vanna turn letters. We behave during "Wheel of Fortune." Jeopardy is a different story, but the meal is over by then.

Sally Bellerose

WHAT IS POLITICALLY CORRECT?

I'M A VEGETARIAN NOT BECAUSE I
LOVE ANIMALS BUT BECAUSE I
HATE PLANTS.

Kris Kovick

Nina Paley

Diet Tips for the Economically Recessed

Was your job thrown out the door when the budget was cut? Worried about the escalating economy? High price of life and food got you down? Well, I can't solve all your problems but I'm here to offer a modest proposal: a simple yet effective system that will help you do as I did and fill your stomach when you don't have a dime in your pocket.

Eat the Rich! The Rich are simply packed with nutrients. And because they're bred in a rarified atmosphere of privilege you needn't worry about excess additives clogging up your system. Like most exclusive health foods the Rich can be hard to find, but the IRS knows exactly where they are. Once you know what you're looking for chances are you can find some right there under your nose.

So when you can't tighten your belt without fainting, remember my advice: *Ask for work. If they won't give you work, ask for bread. If they won't give you bread — Eat the Rich!*

Terry Galloway

Roz Chast

Rina Piccolo

It's Not Hard to Lose Weight

For some baffling reason, mothers regularly ply the most dreadful programs for weight control on their teenage daughters, the world's most vulnerable and least truly needy group of dieters. My mother, an afficionada of the well-balanced diet, proclaimed in 1972, "It's not hard to lose weight. You just eat no sugar, no carbohydrates, and half of everything else."

At which proclamation, my little brother made himself useful for the first time in his life.

"But there is nothing else," he said.

Elizabeth Alexander
excerpt from *The Mind-Tongue Connection*

Kris Kovick

Three Ways to Think of Chocolate

(1) As a reward for having done something good

(2) As a consolation for having done something bad

(3) As a diversion from not having done anything at all.

Pamela Pettler
excerpt from *The Joy of Stress*

Joann Palanker

Jennifer Berman

My Cup of Tea

I often lose my cup of tea
walking from room to room.
I do not know why this should be.
I often lose my cup of tea.
I have a good forgettery.
I also lose the spoon.
I often lose my cup of tea
walking from room to room.

Lillian Morrison

Jackie Urbanovic

Marian Henley

"WELL IF YOU DON'T LIKE THE CASSEROLE, I'LL FREEZE IT AND SAVE IT FOR MY SECOND HUSBAND!"

Martha Campbell

bodies

Flash Rosenberg

Jan Eliot

155

EVEN LARGE GROWN-UP HAIRY MACHO MEN CAN'T FACE:

FEMALE PROBLEMS!

Watch as a small band of courageous red-blooded males witness these **UNSPEAKABLE HORRORS:**

She inserts a diaphragm **RIGHT BEFORE YOUR EYES!** (and then takes it OUT!)

Female reproductive anatomy and the (gulp) **MENSTRUAL CYCLE** explained in **LURID DETAIL!**

Find out what women **REALLY** do with those douche bags! (You'll never be the same!)

A peek at some of the **STRANGER** things you'll see in the typical **LADIES ROOM!**

PLUS: MORE THINGS YOU'D REALLY RATHER NOT HAVE TO THINK ABOUT:

SEE:

MYSTERIOUS APPARATUSES!

HEAR:

I thought I'D NEVER STOP bleeding!

CRAMPS

Ovary

That darn contraceptive sponge was stuck inside me!

PAP SMEAR

Yeast infection

Fallopian tubes!

BLOODCURDLING SOUNDS!

ALSO:

- Bizarre body fluids!
- Unnameable secretions!
- "That" time of the month!
- Vaginitis!
- Feminine itching!

© 1990 Roberta Gregory

Roberta Gregory

Rina Piccolo

Nicole Hollander

Big Breasts!!

Bigger breasts in 90 days or your money cheerfully refunded!

R.T. of Sacramento writes: "My breasts, formerly the size of chickpeas, are now the size of watermelons! Am I thrilled!"

R.W. of Fayetteville writes: "My breasts, formerly the size of roses, are now the size of the Grand Canyon! Am I confused!"

E.Y. of Boston writes: "My breasts, formerly the size of wastebaskets, are now the size of nuclear reactors! Am I hallucinating?"

What does breast size have to do with anything you ask?

Important scientific studies indicate that the larger a woman's breasts, the more likely that men will notice her. A woman who has breasts the size of Xerox machines, for instance, will be more likely to be noticed than a woman whose breasts are only the size of robins' eggs.

What can you do about this?

You can buy our product, which, in moments, will allow you to adjust the size of your own breasts to remarkable proportions.

How easy is it? Does it hurt?

It's fairly complicated, but the results are worth it. No, it doesn't hurt much. Well, it hurts a little, but aren't hooters the size of fireplugs worth a little pain and suffering?

Don't hestitate!

This offer is only good until the attorney general closes us down.

Send your check or money order today!

Roz Warren

"Breasts"

Eve,
I believe,
Was the first to receive.

Emily Newland

For Women Only:
Breast Self-Examination

1. Lie on your back, left hand behind head.

2. With your right hand, examine your left breast. It's awfully lumpy in there, isn't it? Are you sure that's just regular breast tissue? What about here—and here—and—It is! It's a lump! Yes! A lump!

3. With your left hand, wipe sweat off forehead.

Pamela Pettler
excerpt from *The Joy of Stress*

Anne Gibbons

Annie Lawson

SYLVIA

Nicole Hollander

Cath Jackson

Gail Machlis

Barbara Brandon

SHORT- SIGHTED

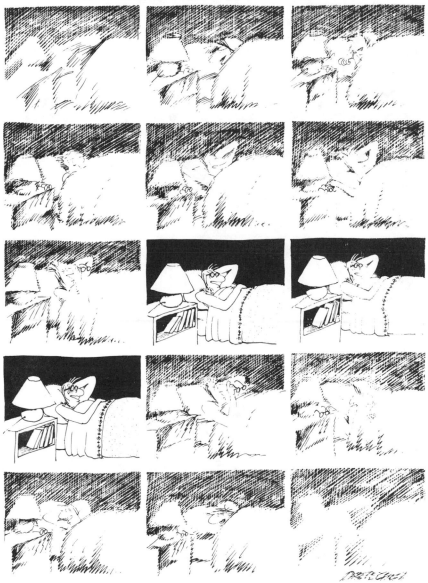

Claire Bretecher

Premenstrual moments...

Ursula Roma

Nina Paley

L.S. Welsh

A Brief History of the Australian Fly Swatter

I traveled over 2,000 miles on a barge down the Congo River, and only encountered one major hurdle: immigration in Zaire. This gave dozens of people, some who appeared to have just walked off the street, the chance to go through all of my belongings, requesting small tokens as they spotted them. "Oh, a mosquito coil? May I have it?" "Oh, a pen. May I have it?" "Oh, a T-shirt. May I have it?" I was led to a room labled "Anti-fraud unit" where an exceedingly burly fellow said he'd rip my pack apart if I didn't donate 50 Zaires, about a dollar. He then proposed marriage. "No," I said. "My father won't allow me to marry you even if you give him twenty cows, five goats, and a car."

He went through my pack. The first compartment he searched held my six-month supply of tampons (there *are* certain niceties of the western world that one does not want to do without, after all).

"What are these?" he barked.

I am shy and easily embarrassed, so I meekly said, "They're for women."

"Yes, but what are they for?"

"They're for women...men don't need them." He still wasn't satisfied and went on to search my day pack, and now came upon my *emergency* supply of tampons (one never knows when and where the need will strike).

"So many," he said. "Are you selling them? What exactly are they for?" I was beginning to worry that he wanted me to demonstrate their use, when Susan, the friend I was traveling with, spoke up. "Here, I'll show you what they're used for," she said and proceeded to tie them onto her hat so that they hung down around her face. "It's an old Australian technique for keeping away flies," she said. I could've died, but this seemed to satisfy my interrogator. He asked if he could have some, and stamped our papers.

I bought us a large bottle of Primus Beer. Susan was still wearing her hat so I took my beer up to her brim and dunked several of the tampons in the glass. As they expanded I said: "Now, if you wear that hat back in Australia, you'll keep away more than just the flies."

Theresa McCracken

Arja Kajermo

Shary Flenniken

168

motherhood

Barbara Brandon

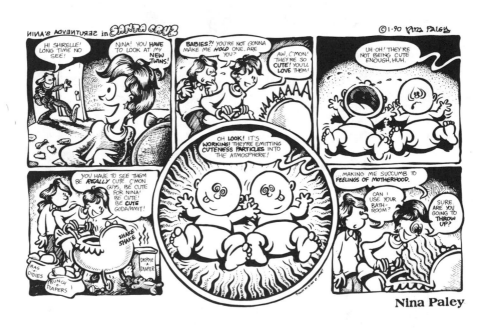

Nina Paley

THE GROWTH OF A FETUS

ONE (1) MONTH
The brain, spinal cord, and nervous system are established. A premature face is forming, including eyes, ears, and mouth, but, by and large, it is all a mess.

TWO (2) MONTHS
The digestive system is well-developed, and already the fetus has acquired a taste for some of the milder cheeses.

THREE (3) MONTHS
The fetus is aware of its own name and is curious about the world around it. It shows a keen interest in the lives of the nearby kidneys and large intestine.

FOUR (4) MONTHS
The fetus is becoming more independent of the mother. Often it will refuse to keep the same hours as the mother, or to hold the same political views. Also, the fetus develops wings, which will disappear by the sixth month.

FIVE (5) MONTHS
The fetus measures ten inches long and is getting sick and tired of standing on its head.

SIX (6) MONTHS
The fetus decides to take up Spanish in its spare time. It sends away for language tapes and books.

SEVEN (7) MONTHS
The fetus is capable of having sex but decides against it.

EIGHT (8) MONTHS
The fetus takes a vacation.

CHILDBIRTH
NINE (9) MONTHS
The fetus starts to plan for the future. It considers money market funds, but wants something less risky at this stage. **Patricia Marx**

171

Unmarried Victorian Lady, Photographed Among Ruins

Minnie went sailing up the Nile
and sketched the ruins in her journal.
She took disasters with a smile
and merely called the heat "infernal."

Her sister married and became
enmeshed in life's domestic trammels,
while Minnie weathered hurricanes
and managed crews of Moors and camels.

Her mother kept the parlor filled
with guests and tea and flower painting.
She spoke of Minnie with distilled
regret and mild attempts at fainting.

Her sister bore a seventh child
and vowed that Min was quite inhuman,
while Minnie breezed along the Nile
and missed fulfillment as a woman.

Gail White

Roz Warren

Jan Eliot

Anne Gibbons

The Emptied Nest Syndrome

Thanks to Oprah, Sally Jesse and scores of articles in newspapers and magazines, I thought I was prepared for the empty nest syndrome.

When my children were 10 and 11, I dreaded the thought that some day they would leave me alone; however, after surviving their teenage years, I became more accepting of the fact that one day I would have the house all to myself.

In fact, by high school graduation, I embraced the empty nest as warmly as an old friend. I think the kids understood when I invited their friends' parents over for a P.T.A. card burning party.

The psychologists have it all wrong. The empty nest does happen when the kids leave home, but it's not an emotional crisis, it's a material one. Let me explain what the term empty nest really means.

The first Saturday morning after my kids left for college, my friend Besty came over for a cup of coffee.

"Why are you wearing that raggedy old bathrobe and when did you start drinking instant coffee?" she asked.

"This is the only bathrobe left in the house and I had to scrounge it from the bag I had packed for the church rummage sale. If it had been hanging in the closet it would have gone, too. I'm drinking instant coffee because my coffee pot has gone to college. Maybe it will learn to make demitasse after its education," I added dryly.

Besty began to look around. She was beginning to understand my situation. "They've really wiped you out. There's no TV, no radio, no clocks."

"You should see the devastation in the bathroom. I don't have any makeup or hairblower and the worst was showering and shampooing without soap and shampoo. Of course, having hot water for the first time in six years was a glorious experience. I almost didn't mind having to drip dry. I think there may be one towel that fell behind the hamper that I can press into service."

Besty doesn't have any children so she really didn't understand the full impact of the situation. "Oh well, you can just go shopping and buy all new things. It's about time you had a set of matching towels anyway."

"Besty, you don't understand. All my money went to college, too. In fact, I may not pay the loans off until my next incarnation."

"You can always use fantastic plastic."

She saw my head lowering like a defeated woman.

"Didn't they leave you anything, anything at all?"

"Yes, I have the dog to feed, the yard to mow and the garbage to carry out."

Besty comes from strong southern stock. "You know, those living room drapes would make a beautiful bathrobe," she suggested.

Brenda Lawlor

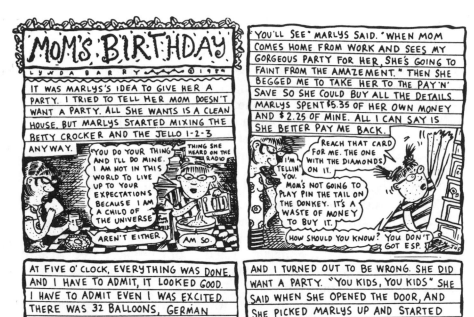

Lynda Barry

childhood

Kris Kovick

Christine Roche

Being a Butterfly

"What are you going to be when you grow up?"

My favorite question. Everyone over a certain height asked it. You'd think the whole world turned on what Allegra Maud Goldman was going to *be* when she grew up. I never gave the same answer twice.

"A gentleman farmer," I said to Mrs. Oxfelder, who was helping me into a blue butterfly dress with big gauze wings. She was about to give me my first dancing lesson.

"Ha, ha," said Mrs. Oxfelder, not unkindly. "You can't be a gentleman farmer, Allegra. You're a girl."

"I'm going to change," I said. A girl was something else I was beginning to learn I might be stuck with, and it was not the best thing to be. I had an older brother, David, and he was something it was better to be. He was a boy. He had a bicycle.

"Wouldn't you like to be a dancer?" Mrs. Oxfelder said. "A lovely, graceful vision, music for the eye, making all the people sigh and dream and weep and cry *bravo?*"

"No."

"Perhaps you'll change your mind," she said, leading me by the hand into a large room where I stood shivering among a lot of other butterflies, some of them fat.

"This is Allegra, girls, our newest *danseuse.*" She sat down at the piano and played a few arpeggios. "Now, girls, I am going to play some airy spring music and I want you to listen to it. Then I want you to think of yourselves as lovely butterflies, free and joyous in the beautiful sunlit sky. And remember, the delicious flowers are blooming everywhere."

She played and the girls started to flit about, flapping their arms and sucking on imaginary flowers. I couldn't believe my eyes. I clamped them shut and threw myself onto the floor, where I lay spread-eagled. The music abruptly ceased.

"Allegra! What kind of butterfly is that?"

"A dead one in a glass case in the Museum of Natural History," I muttered.

Edith Konecky
excerpt from *Allegra Maud Goldman*

My Son Colby

It's taken my son Colby four years, but he's finally reached the amount of weight I gained when I was pregnant. I guess I actually expected him to be about thirty pounds at birth and allow me to lose the other four pounds gracefully, in about a week.

It was all Cecile's fault, of course. When I was pregnant she stuffed me with broccoli drowning in cheese sauce and oranges. This combination had some sort of ultimate vitamin factor, at least according to Cecile. I ate it so dutifully, I expected the baby to be green and orange. I also expected a girl. Girls ran in our families and in our politics. We didn't even have a boy's name picked out. So, while the incredibly heterosexual midwife was pretending that it was business as usual, Cecile was rummaging through the refrigerator, thinking quickly. She came back with the name Colby.

"At least the cheese in the refrigerator wasn't muenster," she'd say later.

Ruthann Robson
excerpt from *Cecile*

Kathryn Lemieux

WE WANT A BELLA ABZUG, A HELEN
CALDICOTT AND A BISHOP TUTU DOLL.

bülbül

cathy by Cathy Guisewite

TOYS

BOYS' — GIRLS'

ARE WE SHOPPING FOR A LITTLE GIRL OR A LITTLE BOY TODAY?

WE'RE SHOPPING FOR A LITTLE UNISEX PERSON.

A LITTLE UNISEX PERSON WHO'D LIKE A DEATH CHARGER ATTACK MISSILE THAT TRANSFORMS INTO A SLIMY MACHINE-GUN MONSTER...

...OR A LITTLE UNISEX PERSON WHO'D LIKE A MAKEUP SET?

A LITTLE UNISEX PERSON WHO'D LIKE A NON-SEX-STEREOTYPED, NON-ROLE-RELATED, NON-GENDER-SPECIFIC GIFT.

VOILÁ! THE DINOSAUR!

PERFECT!

THEY MAY HAVE HAD TO GO BACK TO PREHISTORIC TIMES TO FIND IT, BUT THE TOY INDUSTRY FINALLY HAS SOMETHING FOR CHILDREN THAT WON'T LIMIT THEIR EXPECTATIONS FOR THEMSELVES!!

DID YOU WANT THE DINOSAUR IN THE MANIAC DEMOLISHER COMBAT OUTFIT, OR THE DINOSAUR IN THE BALLERINA BRIDESMAID OUTFIT?

Cathy Guisewite

181

Nina Paley

Conversations with Joann

I used to really love my teacher, Miss Stone. I looked forward to being in school because of her. She was the best teacher. She really, you know, loved us, I think. You got the feeling she cared about you. She took a personal interest. She was pretty happy, she had a lot of ideas. One time she brought someone to school in a big paper bag, and we had to ask it questions. It turned out to be Ben Franklin, sort of. Then one day she walked in the classroom late, first time ever, and she was just weird. Something wasn't right. She sat down at her desk, and she was, well, just on edge. She told us that we were all in the second grade together, except we'd be moving on and she wouldn't. She would be here forever. Forever! She picked up an eraser and threw it at Patrick Sullivan, and he wouldn't hurt a flea. Then she smoked a cigarette. Right in the classroom! She said, "That's right, kiddies, I smoke." She sat at her desk and she smoked the whole thing and then she smoked another one, and then she walked down the aisle and put the butt in Bea Feeley's inkwell. I finally realized she was stinkin' drunk. I said to Dave—he sits in front of me—I said, "Dave, should we get Walter?" Walter's the janitor. Whenever something goes wrong, Walter's the one you deal with.

Well, we went through a pretty weird day. Sometimes Miss Stone was happy and then she would just bottom out. She'd run into the cloakroom and stay in there for about half an hour. She stayed in there all through reading.

The next day our principal came in and said we would be getting a substitute because Miss Stone had become a substance abuser. (Not to mention the way she was treating us.) And she went to seek help at a substance farm.

So this substitute comes in and *she is old.* O-L-D. She can barely walk. The smallest steps you've ever seen. It's almost like she's skating but very slowly and not on skates. Finally she sits down and everybody starts throwing things. We slammed our desktops up and down. She didn't do a thing. Nothing. How could she, at that age. She just sat there. Did you ever see a yogurt-covered raisin? That's what she looked like. Very, very wrinkly and white. She was a mass of age. She sat there for a while. Nothing...

Then she like whispered, "Do art...do art..." Do art? She didn't know anything. So we started up again, someone's lunch went flying across the room, a hard-boiled egg came out. That was a mess, but very funny. I think it was Dolan's. And then Lynna Ardilla puked. Just like that. The whole room just stopped. The substitute teacher, she does nothing of course. And Lynna, who I hate—I don't know why, I just hate her, I just do, everybody hates her—she acts like it didn't happen. She's ignoring it. Puke is dripping off her geography book! Onto the floor. And she's like, gone. Not there at all.

I said, "Lynna, this happened. This has happened. Face it!"

But she didn't look at me. And I know how that goes. You're sitting there, everything is going well, you feel fine, and then, you puke. And part of you just leaves. But no one was doing anything. The whole classroom was stinking. We just sat there. Some people started laughing, so I said, "Dave, you better get Walter."

So Dave left and came back with Walter and Walter was mad. He had a big bag of sawdust and he starts throwing it all over Lynna. All over her! Walter said, "You kids are animals!" Then he left. And there was Lynna, sawdust sticking to her face. Well, we returned to our workbooks. Things were getting back to normal. About ten minutes later I looked up at the teacher, and suddenly her head went down. WHAP! Like that. She was dead. Just like that. I guess it was bound to happen, but you know it takes you by surprise anyway. So...I sat in the front and could see her eyes. They looked like goldfish. I turned to Dave and said, "Dave, you better get Walter."

So Dave left. Walter came in, looked at the teacher, looked at us.

He said, "Who did this?"

Nobody, you know. Nobody did it. It just happened. Somebody yelled out, "Are you gonna use the sawdust?" That did it. Now he was really mad. That got him. He lifted up this old teacher, behind her arms like, and he dragged her out, real fast. Fshshshshshshshshsh...one of her shoes came off, he just left it there. Poor Walter...

We sat in there for the longest time until finally Miss McGreedy came in.

"Boys and girls, resume your work," she said. "And try to act like human beings!" Then she left us there, with our workbooks, with that shoe on the floor. Nobody talked for the rest of the day. It was weird, how a shoe could be in charge.

I like to watch TV. I learn a lot. I still watch Mr. Rogers. I know people make fun of him. I'm aware of that. And I understand it, I do. But he's so...lonely. That's why I watch. I mean, your heart just goes out, you know. He...he has nothing. I mean, he comes home, he opens up that closet, there's nothing there. He only has one sweater and he has to tell the world. He makes such a big deal out of it, it's sad. And then he has to change his shoes. You know why? Because he has only two pairs. That's why he makes such a big deal out of that. He puts on these—I don't know what they are. They aren't like Nikes or Reeboks, they're not the good kind of gym shoes. They're black and they're flat on the bottom. No tread. That's why he walks that way, so carefully. He's not getting any suction.

And he has no real friends. Everyone who comes over is educational. They're there to teach and get out. And his house—barely a picture on the wall. I think the whole place is in black and white.

Not like Pee Wee's house. Pee Wee's got everything. His house is *alive!* You open that refrigerator, the food dances. He's got a chair that jumps every time you say the magic word. He's got a live head in a box with a turban on, a friend who's a cowboy, a bike that flies! I mean, you go to Mr. Roger's, he's talking to the mailman and the mailman wants to leave, he wants out. Here's a grown man who really believes his neighborhood is that miniature town. He *really* thinks he came from there.

Mr. Rogers likes to go out to the kitchen. He says, "Let's go to the kitchen!" Oh, boy, I can't wait. I know there's nothing out there either. But he is truly excited about it. That's why you feel so sorry for him. You go out to his kitchen and he picks up a bowl of fruit, and he takes an orange in his hand, and he says, "This is an orange." I don't think he's aware of what's going on on other channels. I don't think he even has a TV. You can click away and come back later and he'll be peeling that orange. It's pathetic, but how can you turn your back on him?

After I watch Mr. Rogers, I like to see the "Wild Wild World of Animals." This is my favorite show. Have you seen this show? It's not easy to watch. It's, um...every time I watch it something gets eaten, you know. It puts you on edge. There's a voice, a calm voice, like Mr. Roger's. It's in charge. And it's looking down over everything. It's looking down on a bunch of moose. The voice says,

> *This is a herd of reindeer elk.*
> *They are running, running, running*
> *to get away from the long winter ahead.*
> *The herd is fast,*
> *but not every moose will make it.*

As soon as this voice says this, sure enough one of these moose slows down. Whatever this voice says happens, believe me. So this moose starts slowing down. He's got a leg problem and he starts looking back and I'm saying, "Do not look back now, fix it later, get going. Whatever it is, it's not worth it!"

> *In this terrain there are often wild bears,*
> *hungry bears, hunting for slow weak game.*

Sure enough, as soon as he says this, a bear is in the bushes. And, he sees this moose and he looks at him for a while and I'm thinking, Why doesn't somebody stop this? *I* know what's going to happen. But the man is very calm, and he says,

The bear has spotted the moose.
He will be patient with his prey...

And then this bear takes off and you have never seen something going so fast and this moose sees this bear and he tries to run and he looks ahead but the other mooses are long gone. They are not waiting for him, they don't even know who he is. So the bear is catching up to the moose, and I'm thinking, do something! Do something! Throw down a big piece of meat or a tire or something, anything! I know somebody's up there, but they're not saying anything anymore. The voice is, like, out for a sandwich. The bear's got the moose by the antlers and the moose is kicking and his legs are flying up he's struggling struggling struggling he won't stop struggling. He must be pretty out of it. He should play dead and then when the bear stops to look, he should run away. But finally this moose is, well...he's very still.

I...I don't feel happy. But I feel...relieved. And I just hate this bear. I do. From the bottom of my heart, I hate him. The bear looks around to see if anybody saw what he did. But nobody did. At least he doesn't get that satisfaction. He's proud of what he did!

The man's voice comes back, very calm,

The brown bear is proud of her conquest,
now she can feed her hungry cubs.

And then you see the cutest little cubs you have ever seen. And I remember that I love bears, I have a couple of bears myself, and for a minute I forget all about that moose.

The bear cubs come running over, and they gather around the moose, like a dinner table, and they eat the moose. Right on TV! And I remember this show I saw on nature where a moose jumped out of the forest and attacked a herd of sled dogs and killed every one of them. And I'm thinking, maybe this is the same moose. Maybe he got a dose of his own medicine. But I can't be sure...

Overall, the show makes me sick. But for some reason I keep watching.

Nora Dunn

THINGS *NOT* TO TELL YOUR KID

Sometimes we drink milk from cows and sometimes we drink milk from horses like the ones in Central Park.

"The Wizard of Oz" is a true story.

There's a big stopper at the bottom of the ocean, and every once in a while, it gets accidentally pulled out.

Anything electrical can suddenly BLOW UP for no reason whatsoever.

Roz Chast

HOW TO KEEP CHILDREN QUIET FOR HOURS

CONNECT THE DOT

Rina Piccolo

"NO, SHE WASN'T A LATCHKEY CHILD. SHE WAS A HOUSEBREAKER."

Martha Campbell

lesbiana

Jackie Urbanovic

Cath Jackson

Truth, Justice and the Lesbian Way

Faster than a speeding Harley...
More powerful than a leather-clad butch...
Able to leap tall homophobes in a single bound...
Look! Up in the air—
It's a bird...it's a plane...it's Super Dyke!

Super Dyke.

Man, the things I would do if I were Super Dyke.

First of all, I wouldn't say "man." I'd say "goddess" and not feel self-conscious about it.

If I were Super Dyke and a co-worker told a "faggot" joke, I wouldn't bury my head in my hands (as I'm tempted to do) and mumble to myself, "I gotta get another job." Nor would I settle for meekly saying (as I generally do), "I don't appreciate that kind of humor."

Hell, no! If I were Super Dyke, I'd jump up from my chair, leap onto the table and rip open my shirt, exposing my deep lavender Super Dyke suit, complete with tights, cape and a hot pink "D" emblazoned across the chest. "I am Super Dyke," I'd tell the joker, "and I will not stand for such bigotry. Not only does it spread hate and ignorance, but such outright stupidity is an embarrassment to all of us who work with you."

If that didn't shut him up, I'd turn his ears purple.

Of course, if I were Super Dyke I wouldn't be in a corporate job. I'd work for a non-profit agency that educated women about breast cancer , or investigated toxic waste dumping, or provided legal defense for lesbians in child custody cases. Maybe all three.

If I were Super Dyke, I'd march with Queer Nation, protest with ACT-UP, be on the speaker's bureau for P-FLAG. I'd belong to dozens of lesbian and gay organizations—NGLTF, LHA, MCC, GCN, HRCF—*and* I'd know what all the initials stood for.

Basically, if I were Super Dyke, I wouldn't put up with so much crap from rich, white guys. I'd walk right up to the owners of all the big hotels in town, look them right in the eye and say, "You make this hotel wheelchair accessible or I'll kill you." I'd fly over "Operation Rescue" terrorist Randall Terry and drop a bag of ripe compost on his head. I'd convince the editors at the *Saturday Evening Post* to start a scholarship fund for gay teenagers. I'd make Cardinal Cook tithe his annual salary to Planned Parenthood.

Yup, if I were Super Dyke, no gay-bashers, anti-semites or racists would dare cross my path. Educators and religious leaders, however, would seek me out for advice and consultation, which I would give freely. Yes, I would do this despite my full-time job at the non-profit agency, twelve hours weekly of volunteer work, two nights of classes and my every other Thursday evening Eco-feminism reading group.

You see if I were Super Dyke, I'd have my personal shit together too. I'd overcome my white, upper-middle class anxiety and live in a racially mixed, economically diverse neighborhood with people of all ages. We'd have community meetings where we'd work on our racist, classist, ageist, ableist, sizeist and heterosexist issues. On the weekends we'd work together in our community garden.

If I were Super Dyke, I'd bike to work, eat organic food, write to my elected officials and buy books from small publishing houses. I'd learn Spanish and American Sign Language, dialog with my bisexual friends, reclaim my Judaism. I'd meditate, do tai-chi, go to full-moon chants and, unless I received inner-guidance to speak, I'd sit in quiet contemplation at Quaker meetings.

If I were Super Dyke, I'd know my Mary Daly, Sonia Johnson and Audre Lorde inside out. I'd subscribe to OutLook, OutWeek, and BlackOut, and I'd make time to read them all.

If I were Super Dyke, I'd boycott Coca-Cola, Burroughs-Wellcome and Domino's pizza. I wouldn't drink Coors beer, El Salvadorean coffee or Nestle's Quik but I wouldn't go around feeling morally superior to those who did. (Not outwardly, at least.)

I'd avoid anything plastic.

Yeah, if I were Super Dyke, I'd be out-going yet inward-seeking, assertive yet sensitive, intellectual yet funny. I'd always return my phone messages, write to my great-aunt monthly, grow my own herbs, recycle my paper bags, eat up the leftovers before they grew mold, change the cat box more often and of course, make wild, passionate, artful and tender love with my devoted partner of fourteen years.

Yes, if I were Super Dyke...I'd probably give myself an ulcer. Or even a heart attack.

High-blood pressure at the very least.

So maybe I don't need to be Super Dyke. Maybe I don't *have* to do everything. Maybe instead of Super Dyke, I could be Pretty-Good Dyke, starting out with a handful of these things and move up slowly. With forethought, with sincerity, with dedication.

And maybe that is super enough all by itself.

Ellen Orleans

Jennifer Camper

IMAGINE PERFECT PARENTS, WHO TOTALLY
ACCEPTED YOU AS YOU ARE. YOU'D STILL NEED
THERAPY, ALTHOUGH FOR DIFFERENT REASONS.

Kris Kovick

194

Letters from Home

I don't know if this happens to any of you...but I'll write my parents a letter filled with thoughts, emotions, feelings, questions, concerns, certainties, uncertainties, and I'll get a letter back, addressing *nothing* I wrote about in the letter. Usually it's something like this:

Dear Lisa,
How are you? We're fine. The weather's been nice. We played tennis yesterday and spoke to Aunt Marilyn. How's your job? Are you eating well? Please write soon.
Love,
Mom & Dad

...So, I decided on a new tactic. From now on, when I write my parents a letter, I also include a copy of the letter I'd *like* to receive from them, ask them to sign it, and send it back. Here's the latest one I've sent:

Dear Lisa,
We were just telling some of our friends in our PFLAG group—Parents and Friends of Lesbians & Gays—how *happy* we are for you that you came out of the closet. We are just *so* proud of who you are. "My daughter is a lesbian!" I just *love* to hear myself say those words.

How are you since your recent break-up? Are you seeing any nice Jewish girls? Our neighbor has a daughter we'd *really* like you to meet. And she's a doctor!

We put a lot of thought into what you wrote in your last letter, and you have a really good point. After over 30 years of being a non-communicative family, we're also very glad that we collectively decided to work on interpersonal relations within the immediate family. We'd *love* to come visit you in San Francisco and see your life there. We support you in *everything* you do.
Love,
Mom & Dad
P.S. How's your job? Are you eating well?

Lisa Geduldig

STONEWALL RIOTS

Andrea Natalie

"I hope you don't expect any eggs from me. I'm a lesbian."

Christine Roche

therapy

ON READING FREUD

Cath Jackson

Therapy Paranoia

I've talked to other people, so I know it isn't just me. I think I see my shrink's car everywhere. It's terrifying, like she's multiplying at an incredible rate. I memorized her license number just to avoid becoming paranoid. But every time I see a car with the wrong plates that looks like hers, I check to see who's driving it. And when it isn't her, I'm still not convinced. Even when it's some fat old man, and my shrink is as far from that as you can get, I think I'm suppressing painful information and hallucinating her into some other person's body. She could be driving any car on the road. I don't know why my shrink needs to drive a car at all. She gets under my skin faster than the speed of light.

Lorrie Sprecher

200

Alison Bechdel

Claire Bretecher

Roz Chast

C'Mon already,
snap out of it —
we **ALL** had
lousy childhoods.

Oh, I have problems —
but they're always
'HAPPY
PROBLEMS'!

Mary Lawton

Sharon Rudahl

Marlan Henley

Jennifer Berman

work

Marian Henley

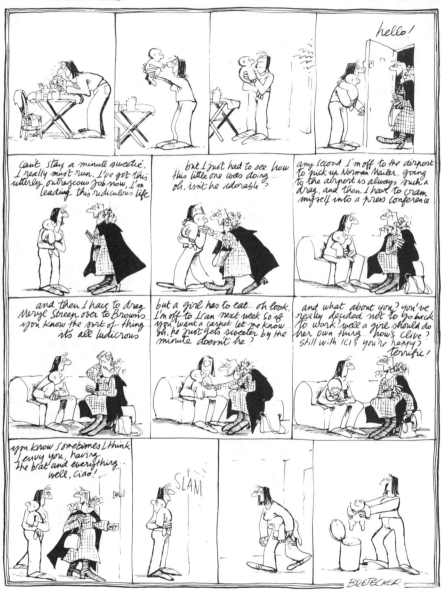

Claire Bretecher

Private Sessions Available

I'm very pleased and proud to be addressing the Northeast Regional Chapter of the Aspiring American Small Businesswoman's Information Exchange Support Group Network Luncheon. Especially because you're down there in last year's clothes and I'm up here in a new haircut and color rinse looking like a million and just back from a very expensive vacation.

Last year, I was on your side of the podium. You may find it hard to believe, looking at me now, but I haven't forgotten what I went through, and I'm here today to share my journey, hoping in that way to share strategies, empowerment and hope.

When I lost my job—just like most of you—after six months of unemployment, it seemed the only thing I still knew how to do was to follow up employment leads and rewrite my resume. So building on my painfully acquired expertise, I made the obvious move, and became a career counselor. So did thousands of other unemployed women. How many of you out there call yourself career development consultants? Transitional employment specialists? How many of you are as broke as I used to be?

I hit bottom. It happened one day during the spring of 1991 when a woman sat across from me and criticized my efforts on her behalf, completely undermining my already significantly damaged self-esteem. "You're supposed to be the expert," she said. "You're supposed to spot trends and recognize needs, position me for opportunities before they're even open. You're doing a lousy job." At first, I felt diminished, then enraged to have this unemployed supplicant who couldn't even write her own resume telling me how to run my business. But then it hit me: she was right. In that moment—when I could have given up—instead I had my idea.

I looked her straight in the eye and asked, "How would you like to be President of Iraq?"

"What?" she said. "I'm an American. An American *woman.*" I carefully maintained eye-contact. "Besides," she said, "I'm Jewish."

Months of unemployment make a person prone to negativity and this client was no exception. It became second nature to see why a thing won't work instead of exploring ways to make it happen. Are we all Americans here in the audience? Well, then, tell me, is it permissible to include religion on a resume? No, of course not. And hiring based on gender— why, that's the sort of un-American nonsense promoted by those supporters of quotas and equal opportunity, so-called, who fortunately have been so thoroughly discredited by now their clamor can be entirely ignored. So, I told her, forget the Jewish woman stuff. As for being an American, who do you think is going to choose and impose the next ruler of Iraq anyway? I mean, it should be clear to absolutely everyone that Saddam can't last forever and a democratic regime will have to take his place. But, hey, it's Iraq, it can't be all that democratic. I mean people aren't actually going to vote, are they?

My client showed an immediate stirring of interest. But almost as immediately her impaired self-confidence got in the way, working in tandem with her societally programmed need to fail. She defensively began to raise objections, such as, "I have no government experience"—this from a woman who's been running a household for almost twenty years! and— even more lamely—"I don't speak Arabic."

No problem. She didn't have to speak Arabic. She was applying to run the country, not a talk show. Besides, if she wanted, all we had to do was include fluency in the language on her resume. Was this dishonest? Not at all. Because as some of you have probably already realized, we had no place to send this resume anyway. But consider: if we'd prepared a legitimate c.v., scrupulously documenting her educational background and years of experience as a financial analyst, we *still* would have had nowhere to send it.

Fantasy is what gives me the edge in the fast-growing competitive field of white collar professional unemployment. Other counselors only set their clients up for disappointment. What's the point, where's the satisfaction, in preparing straightforward factual genuine applications for jobs that—realistic as they seem—don't actually exist? When the people who might have been hiring are now all bankrupt, on trial, or unemployed just like you? My clients, on the other hand, walk out of my office carrying a power resume: 500 copies typeset from computer and run off on high quality, 25% rag content, 20-pound ivory bond—describing them as they'd *like* to be, setting professional goals that reflect their dreams, not the corporate-ladder compromises most of us have settled for all of our adult working lives.

I give a woman a chance to change her life—on paper. I compose appropriate educational and professional backgrounds and every client has my iron-clad guarantee that any name listed as a reference will have a celebrity recognition factor of at least 85%.

Am I really making money? All right, so I'm a little overextended on my credit cards, but the economy needs consumer confidence and what else can you do when you're starting a new business and can't get a bank loan? Have any of my clients been dissatisfied? I'll be honest—you can't please everyone, there's always some grumblers and naysayers and malcontents and I'll be the first to admit that I made my share of mistakes when I was starting out. One of them was a whopper: I actually encouraged one of my more desperate clients to apply for a position that at the time was going begging: Democratic candidate for President. She was so offended, she got up from my kitchen table and walked right out the door. Even for a shoo-in job, she could not align herself with the losers who want to tax the rich and coddle the failures. She stood up for the American Dream.

Which is what we all have to do. My own experience proves that thanks to today's Republican culture, even with the demise of opportunities in S&L's and junk bonds, business in the non-productive sector is better than ever. You can still strike it rich in the wonderful new world of economic fantasy.

Before we close so that I can get to my health club appointment, I want to ask something of each of you. Make a commitment to yourself. Take responsibility—now—for creating your own success. There's a little exercise I want you all to try at home, tonight and every night. All you have to do is repeat a simple little phrase. Stand in front of the mirror. Look yourself right in the eye and then say it in your strong and beautiful voice: *I am somebody else!* Why be yourself when it's the other people who get all the breaks? *I am somebody else!* How about a little louder? With a little more conviction? *Somebody*—please, God!—*somebody else!*

Diane Lefer

Christine Roche

What Should You Do if Your Boss Propositions You?

Theoretically, there is no problem here. Freud said the well-adjusted person is one who is happy in both love and work, but this could have been just a line Freud used with his female patients.

Freud had many other clever little tricks—like transference—which he used to make women fall in love with him. You should be on guard against these tricks, for if you succumb to Freud's charms and have an affair with him, you will never get better. Tell him you respect his work, especially on dream interpretation, and agree that an affair would be convenient, but that he reminds you of your father, and you are afraid your mother would feel left out. Freud will understand.

If you do not work for Freud, just say no.

Patricia Marx

Cath Jackson

'Er, Sir, I'm worried that working with these, um, chemicals may be affecting my short-term memory'

'Don't forget, Perkins, that I'm working here too. What about my short-term memory?'

'What about it, Sir?'

'What about what, Perkins?'

Ros Asquith

Shary Flenniken

Cath Jackson

© 1982 T.O. SYLVESTER

Where is that memo I asked you to xerox?
I seem to have copies of Chapter 2 from "The Joy of Lesbian Sex."

WE WANT MEN TO BE EQUALLY
PINNED UP ON THE JOB !!

bülbül

Anne Gibbons

Anne Gibbons

guys

"I like the concept of "Men"... It's the reality I have problems with..."

"I'd like to find a man who's sensitive in general, and macho in emergencies."

Anne Gibbons

The Goddess creates men.

Andrea Natalie

THE MODERN THEORY OF THE DESCENT OF MAN

Christine Roche

221

Barbara Brandon

SYLVIA

Nicole Hollander

Marlan Henley

Trash Day

To hell with the bar scene, personal ads, blind dates.....
A superior system for meeting your match exists right before our eyes.
I can't believe we didn't think of it sooner.
In my neighborhood, Tuesday is trash day.
We all set out our stuff
then quietly check each other's discards for something good to take in.
What a great system! And a perfect model for meeting mates.
On Wednesdays, why not leave those we no longer love out on the curb
so our neighbors could pick them up?
It's not rude. It's direct. It's what happens anyway.
You know. You meet someone terrific
and you can't imagine someone else got rid of him,
just like that great cabinet I found....

Flash Rosenberg

Yes, she liked a man who could sweep her off her feet... and afterwards, take out the garbage without complaining...

Stephanie Piro

So Many Petite Virginettes

So many petite virginettes ask, "Oh, Judy, why does my man turn into a pig when another man walks into the room?" Your love thing may be as sweet as pecan pie and submissive as a Play-Doh puppy when he needs food and lodging for his lovelog. But once the wild love beast is satisfied, he has to reinforce his maleness by hooting, howling, and rolling with his piggy pals like a bunch of hardhats humping a virgin.

My own brothers act like this. One on one, they are some of the most precious primates in captivity. For example, my brother Bosco will say, "Judy, I saw you on *Geraldo*, it was great." Then my brother Bingo slithers into the room and they both get possessed by Hoss Cartwright and they yell, "Hey Jude, make us some grub." Right, like the Goddess of Love is gonna get tied to the stove and make pancakes for these plumbers.

And forget it if an unsuspecting pseudovirgin should tie the knot. Your love leech now knows he has a horizontal heifer for life, so he parks in front of the TV and retains beer for the Superbowl, and the only way you're gonna get his attention is to powersnort Chee-tos until you look like the Astrodome.

It must be an unwritten rule that when two or more men get together, they have to assert their extra Y chromosomes to make sure their testosterone is still intact. Let's face facts: It's kind of a minor tip-off that in the reproductive process, all stud puppets contribute is their seed. Oh, thanks, Jack in the Beanstalk. But we fertile femmes are the ones who power-bloat for nine months and give birth to some screaming mass of cells that will one day shoot us for the Mazda.

What ever happened to the kind of love leech that lived in his car and dropped by once a month to throw up and use you for your shower? Now all these pigs want is a *commitment*. It makes me sick. These Alan Alda, family-focused, dead-men-do-eat-quiche hogs all say, "Oh, now that it's the Nineties, we're sensitive. We just want to sit around with a bunch of men and cry." Well, go to a Yankees game! It's tough love.

Now these baby-men want a 1-900-slutsicle, like Jessica Hahn. (Right, like her body was not donated by Du Pont.) Or they want a multimedia bondage goddess like myself to spank them. Like I have time to discipline some sperm whale with a Visa card. Excuse me, you middle-aged minoxidil millionaires, but why can't you figure out that that nude blonde who lives in your jockstrap is working her way up to your wallet?

By now I'm sure you can tell that I'm the kind of cowgirl who sits by the phone and waits for some pig to call. Yeah, dream on, Cling-ons. Like I'm a sucker for any stud who looks like he's one rejection away from sitting on

a sucker for any stud who looks like he's one rejection away from sitting on a rooftop with a rifle. I can't wait to get puffed up by some sanitation worker with a prison record. I like my men the way I like my subways...hot, packed, and unloading every three minutes!

Judy Tenuta

Mary Lawton

Memo:

When I hear some woman say she
has finally decided you can spend time with
other women, I wonder what she means: Her
mother? My mother?
I've always despised my woman friends. Even
if they introduced me to a man I found
attractive I have never let them become
what you could call my intimates. Why
should I? Men are the ones with the money and
the big way with waiters and the passkey
to excitement in strange places of real
danger and the power to make things happen
like babies or war and all these great ideas
about mass magazines for members of the weaker sex
who need permission
to eat potatoes or a doctor's opinion on orgasm after death
or the latest word on what the female
executive should do, after hours, wearing
what. They must be morons: women!
Don't you think?
I guess you could say
I'm stuck in my ways
as
That Cosmopolitan Girl.

June Jordan

Mary Lawton

Roz Chast

So much for penis envy.

Andrea Natalie

Rina Piccolo

Jennifer Berman

Marian Henley

literature

Nina Paley

Is It Okay to Read Someone else's Mail that is Sitting on the Kitchen Table?

Many people believe you should read only that which is written for you. Nonsense. *Road To My Heart* was written "for Debbie, who was always there with a cup of coffee," but nonetheless I, and I think thousands of others, have rightfully enjoyed the novella. Anyone who says it is wrong to read *Road to My Heart* or to read another person's mail advocates censorship. Censorship is morally reprehensible. It is almost as abhorrent as neglecting to open the letter on the table if it is sealed. There may be a notice inside saying the heat will be shut off unless payment is immediately forthcoming. Now, better rifle through the drawers to see if there's any money lying around for the heat.

Patricia Marx

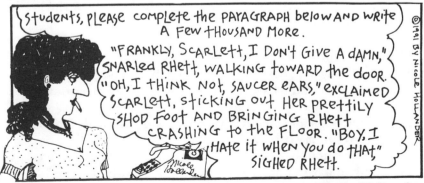

Nicole Hollander

Land of Hopefully and Glory

If the practitioners of Lockjaw Choctaw in our midst had their way, American's most beloved novel would sound like this:

Scarlett O'Hara was not a physically ideal human being but men seldom perceived it when informed by her life-enhancing qualities as the Tarleton twins were.

"What does it matter if we were expelled from the college of our choice, Scarlett? The hostilities are going to start any day now. You don't think we'd pursue career-enrichment opportunities with hostilities in progress, do you?"

"Not going to be any hostilities? Why, honey, after the first-strike shelling situation we instituted at Fort Sumner, the Yankees will have to engage in hostilities. Violence always begets violence."

"If you boys don't address another issue, I'll go in the house and express my rage!"

"How about if we tell you a privileged communication? You know Miss Melanie Hamilton who's based in Atlanta? Ashley Wilke's cousin? They say Ashley's going to marry her. You know the Wilkeses tend to have meaningful relationships with their extended family members."

"Devastating! I'm going to ask Pa if he has any input."

"Do you mean to tell me, Katie Scarlett O'Hara, that you neither advocate nor condone home ownership? Why, home ownership is the only viable alternative worth livin' for, worth fightin' for, worth dyin' for, because it's the only comprehensive program for stage-one social mobility."

"Oh, Pa, you talk like a Hibernian-American."

"'Tis proud I am that I'm Hibernian-American, and don't you be forgettin', Missy, that you're half Hibernian-American, too, and to anyone with a drop of Hibernian blood in him or her, the land he or she lives on is like his or her female parent."

"Ashley, I—I love you."

"You musn't say that, Scarlett. It will serve no useful purpose."

"But Ashley, I know you have felt a need for me. Say you have a felt need for me!"

"I have a felt need for you but it has no growth potential. Oh, Scarlett, can't we put a voluntary ban on these things?"

"Don't you want to have a one-on-one commitment with me?"

"I'm going to have a one-on-one commitment with Melanie."

"But you just said you had a felt need for me!"

"I misspoke. My dear, why must you make me verbalize things that will only give you a negative self-image? You're so young and unformulated that you don't know what a one-on-one commitment means."

"I know that I love you."

"Love isn't enough to construct a positive orientation for two people as polarized as we are. You, who are so autonomous and self-realizing—"

"Why don't you articulate it, you wimp? You're threatened by me! You'd rather live with that submissive little nurturer who can't open her mouth except to say 'affirmative' and 'negative,' and parent a network of passive role players just like her!"

"You musn't say counterproductive things about Melanie. She's part of my gene pool and we interact."

"She's a pale-faced, unassertive ninny and I'm unsupportive of her!"

"As the Supreme Being is my witness, I'm going to effect a take-charge dynamic with a view toward making it unthinkable that I will ever be inadequately nourished again. I'm going to develop survival techniques, and when it's all over, I'll never be disadvantaged again. If I have to harass, victimize, utilize, or practice situation ethics, I'll never be without my basic nutrients at any subsequent point in time."

"Ashley, the Yankees want three hundred dollars to pay the taxes on Tara!"

"Why tell me? You know I can't cope."

"But Ashley, this is a worst-case scenario!"

"What do people do when they're faced with a worst-case scenario? Some are able to initiate direct action to achieve full humanity, while inadequate personalities become victims of the winnowed-out factor."

"Ashley, let's relocate! They need non-combat advisors in the Mexican army. Oh, Ashley, we could have a restructuring experience!"

"I can't leave Melanie. She has no job-training opportunities."

"She has no reproductive capabilities, either, but I could give you—"

"Scarlett, this is totally and categorically unacceptable!"

"Then...we have no options?"

"Nothing, except...self-esteem."

"Rhett, Ashley and I didn't have a meaningful encounter at the lumber yard. We were just building bridges of understanding within a platonic framework."

"Oh, I don't begrudge him recreational sex with you. I can identify with that. Ever since you denied me control over your body, I've reaffirmed myself with surrogates like Belle. But I do begrudge him your consciousness because our value judgements are at same-stage. We could have communicated so well, Scarlett, but I couldn't deal with your insecurities so I bonded with Bonnie instead. I'm into fathering now."

"Promise me?"
"Anything, Melly."
"Look after Ashley for me. See that he gets counseling, he's so unstructured."

"But Rhett, if you leave me, what will I do about re-entry?"
"Frankly, my dear, it doesn't impact me."
"I'll go home to Tara and monitor the situation. I'll think of some way to re-establish connectedness. After all, tomorrow is another time frame!"

As American *l`ese language* goes, the "less calories than" advertisements really aren't so bad. True degeneration is found in the wordsmithery of small, unknown companies who can't afford to hire the best and the brightest. Operating largely through mail orders, they don't advertise on television or in the major print media. The literature that comes with their products sounds like this:

Congratulations! Your purchase of *The Skid Daisy* proves that you are the kind of person that knows what can happen in the bathtub!

The Skid Daisy obsoletes everything else in bathtub caution.

The Skid Daisy is different than other safety-oriented devices.

The Skid Daisy prevents you from a skidding experience as it is designed to totally cover the entire bottom of your bathtub.

The Skid Daisy allows you to leave go of safety bars and use both hands for your shower activity owing to the fact that it's outer surface is treated with invisible suction cups that gently grip your feet, to the naked eye.

The Skid Daisy holds your soap still in the event that you dropped it.

The Skid Daisy decors your whole new bathroom!

The Skid Daisy gives your guests something to talk about!

That's what *The Skid Daisy* is all about!

Directions for installing your *The Skid Daisy*:

1. Open bathroom window! Your *The Skid Daisy* is treated with a special superchemical which impacts irritating nasal membranes if the room is not air-oriented.

2. Center the drain hole opening over your drain hole and peel away sufficient of it's outer protecting layer to expose three or four inches of your *The Skid Daisy* to the bottom of your bathtub, pressing.

3. Continue to repeat until your entire bottom of your bathtub is covered and it's outer protecting layer is completely peeled off.

4. Feel to see if there are any puckers before wetting it with your fingers.

5. If you are not satisfied with your *The Skid Daisy*, write to Pam Parker in our Public Relations Department, or dial 1-800-SKIDNOT, who will address the toll-free problem.

Do not write to Pam Parker unless you want more of the same, because she and the classical stylist who wrote the brochure are one and the same person:

Dear Ms. King:
Firstly, let me say how sorry we were to hear about your experience with regard to your *The Skid Daisy*.

Thank you muchly for the X-ray of your irritating membranes, the photograph of your bathtub, the photograph of your feet, and the other photograph. With this end in view, I have transpired it to our lawyer's, who will formulate an irrespective opinion as to the obligation of your injuries, pertaining.

As you wrote to us previous to the time limit within 30 days of the subsequent purchase agreement to the dead line's running out was up, our warranty gladly inforces us a guarantee to send you a free gift replacement of a new *The Skid Daisy*.

Please advise as to which choice you wish to prefer between the Greek Temples, Tropical Paradise, Arizona Sunset, or our new Chinese-oriented design.

Skidlessly Your's,
Pam

Florence King

An Excerpt from <u>Me</u>: The Unauthorized Autobiography

Friends who had consented to interviews when I first considered an autobiography withdrew their cooperation after discovering the project no longer had my approval. Long before I stopped returning my calls, they understood my motives were suspect. Most, I am happy to report, shredded their depositions and promised me that when and if I gave myself my full cooperation, they would be honored to talk.

Mary Kay Zuravleff

Comparison

Keats was dead at 24—
I expect to reach three-score.

Keats has earned immortal fame—
I'm still dreaming of the same.

Love forsook his lonely sheets—
we're much alike, myself and Keats.

Gail White

Cath Jackson

Codicil

Experts are now fine-combing [William Faulkner's] writings in every stage....They are trying to determine...how—ideally—he wanted his books published.

This posthumous literary revision—known as "authorial intention" or "final intention"—has been advanced by scholars in the last few years....

Punctuation was important to Faulkner to establish mood and thought. When he wanted to indicate introspection, he punctuated the dialogue, in his tightly compressed handwriting, with 6 to 10 dots, like this: . . . . When he wanted to show that something was happening outside the experience of his characters, he often used a long line of dashes, like this: —————
—*The New York Times, June 5, 1985*

Be it understood by my literary executor and his heirs and assigns that the system of punctuation explained hereunder is my posthumous intention; that it applies to each and all of my literary effects, including all and any novels, novellas, novelettes, sprawling narrative panoramas of urban horror, potboilers, and erotic classics, not excluding the "Supervising Nurse" series; and that in the case of any deviation from said system of punctuation whatsoever, howsoever printed, said deviation shall be expunged and replaced by the version that was originally intended all along in the first place.

1) . . . . Eight dots before dialogue indicates that whatever the character says, he or she really means the exact opposite.

2) . . . . + More than eight dots before a dialogue creates a different feeling, more like doubt or distrust. Or maybe the character is just stalling. We don't know. Instead of having the meaning be cut and dried, it's more like: Wait a minute, is this guy on the level or not? That's the realism I depict with the extra dots.

3) //" "// Double slash marks around dialogue reveals that at the very moment this character is talking, somewhere else in the world a volcano is erupting, a war is raging, or somebody of a different race is seeing things from another perspective.

4) (!) An exclamation point in parentheses after dialogue makes it obvious that I, the author, know that what the person just said is really stupid.

5) *&%!*¢#??! An asterisk, ampersand, percent sign, exclamation point, another asterisk, a cent sign, a number sign, two question marks, and a final exclamation point anywhere in dialogue clues the reader in to the fact that the character has a tremendous anger against society.

6) ——————————— A single long dash after dialogue adds a very downbeat note. It's just a little touch I throw in once in a while. For the mood.

7): A colon before the beginning of a paragraph conveys a Wagnerian-overture type of effect. Power! Impact!

8) **********A line of asterisks after a scene with kissing or sex implies another scene with vampirism or more sex.

9) [ ] Material inside a brackets suggests insanity. Maybe one of the characters feels like blowing his top. How do you show this? I want the reader to see those brackets and immediately think: Craziness! Chaos!

10) ;;;;;;;;; A group of semicolons gives an unusual flavor. It's just a hell of an unexpected thing.

11) *Italic print* I use all over the place. This is a bug I have. *Italic print!* I love it. It's for when a first-person or omniscient narrator is probing psychic wounds that will never heal, which I do a lot.

12)————————Six dashes in the middle of nowhere (I thought of using five for this, but then I decided no, six) has the function of blasting emotion out of the uncharted waters of consciousness inside every reader, be he or she a profound philosopher or just an individual of no great brain power, because no matter who you are or what you are, you contain the mysteries of your own subterranean life, your caverns of fear, rage, desire, everything offbeat, all protected by walls of ice until suddenly, smash!— along comes the icemelt into a river of strange sensations, which no one but you is ever supposed to know about. Here is where I touch on the universal problem: that you can never, never go completely into the other guy's heart.

13) A capital letter at the beginning of a sentence is a private joke.

I want these inserted in all my works. There's a list on my bulletin board of where they go.

Veronica Geng

Advice to New Poets

When editors reject you flat,
write a poem about a cat.
If you still receive rejections,
write a poem about erections.
Gail White

Alice Muhlback

Cath Jackson

Song

The world is full of colored
people
People of Color
Tra-la-la
The world is full of
colored people
Tra-la-la-la-la.

They have black hair
and black and brown
eyes
The world is full of
colored people
Tra-la-la.

The world is full of colored
people
People of Color
Tra-la-la
The world is full of colored
people
Tra-la-la-la-la.

Their skins are pink and yellow
and brown
All colored people
People of Color
Colored people
Tra-la-la.

Some have full lips
Some have thin
Full of colored people
People of Color
Colored lips
Tra-la-la.

The world is full of
colored people
People of Color
Colorful people
Tra-la-la!

Alice Walker

CAUCASIAN TRANSLATION

CAMPER

OH, **OF COURSE** YOU'LL BE COMFORTABLE! IT'S A VERY **MIXED** BAR!

TRANSLATION: 3 AFRICAN-AMERICANS, 2 LATINAS, AND 527 WHITE PEOPLE.

I'M NOT RACIST— IN FACT, I'M **VERY** ATTRACTED TO BLACK MEN...

TRANSLATION: ALL MY FRIENDS ARE WHITE, ALL THE MEN I FUCK ARE BLACK.

I'M NOT PREJUDICED. HELL— I GREW UP WITH BLACKS!

TRANSLATION: MY PARENTS HIRED A WEST INDIAN WOMAN TO RAISE THE KIDS.

WHY DOES EVERYBODY HAVE TO LABEL THEMSELVES "AFRICAN-AMERICAN" OR "CHINESE-AMERICAN" OR "MEXICAN-AMERICAN" — CAN'T WE ALL JUST BE **PEOPLE?**

TRANSLATION: CAN'T WE ALL JUST BE WHITE?

Jennifer Camper

Clarity

Mama Day and Grandma had told me that there was a time when the want ads and housing listings in newspapers—even up north—were clearly marked colored or white. It must have been wonderfully easy to go job hunting then. You were spared a lot of legwork and headwork. And how I longed for those times, when I was busting my butt up and down the streets. I said as much at one of those parties Selma was always giving for her certain people. You would've thought I had announced that they were really drinking domestic wine, the place got that quiet. One of her certain people was so upset his voice shook: "You mean, you want to bring back segregation?" I looked at him like he was a fool—where had it gone? I just wanted to bring the clarity about it back—it would save me a whole lot of subway tokens. What I was left to deal with were the ads labeled *Equal Opportunity Employer*, or nothing—which might as well have been labeled *Colored apply* or *Take your chances*. And if I wanted to limit myself to the sure bets, then it was an equal opportunity to be what, or earn what? That's where the headwork came in.

Gloria Naylor
excerpt from *Mama Day*

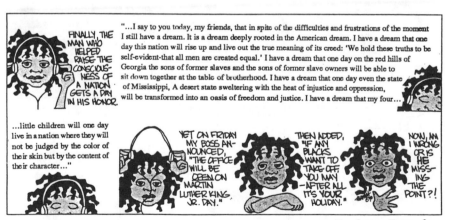

Barbara Brandon

Shary Flenniken

WHITE BOY WITH THE BEET

Kris Kovick

Jennifer Camper

Roz Chast

The Little Hours

Now what's this? What's the object of all this darkness all over me? They haven't gone and buried me alive while my back was turned, have they? Ah, now would you think they'd do a thing like that! Oh, no, I know what it is. I'm awake. That's it. I've waked up in the middle of the night. Well, isn't that nice. Isn't that simply ideal. Twenty minutes past four, sharp, and here's Baby wide-eyed as a marigold. Look at this, will you? At the time when all decent people are just going to bed, I must wake up. There's no way things can ever come out even, under this system. This is as rank as injustice is ever likely to get. This is what brings about hatred and bloodshed, that's what *this* does.

Yes, and you want to know what got me into this mess? Going to bed at ten o'clock, that's what. That spells ruin. T-e-n-space-o-apostrophe-c-l-o-c-k: ruin. Early to bed, and you'll wish you were dead. Bed before eleven, nuts before seven. Bed before morning, sailors give warning. Ten o'clock, after a quiet evening of reading. Reading—there's an institution for you. Why, I'd turn on the light and read, right this minute, if reading weren't what contributed toward driving me here. I'll show it. God, the bitter misery that reading works in this world! Everybody knows that—everybody who *is* everybody. All the best minds have been off reading for years. Look at the swing La Rochefoucauld took at it. He said that if nobody had ever learned to read, very few people would be in love. There was a man for you, and that's what *he* thought of it. Good for you, La Rochefoucauld; nice going, boy. I wish I'd never learned to read. I wish I'd never learned to take off my clothes. Then I wouldn't have been caught in this jam at half-past four in the morning. If nobody had ever learned to undress, very few people would be in love. No, his is better. Oh, well, it's a man's world.

La Rochefoucauld, indeed, lying quiet as a mouse, and me tossing and turning here! This is no time to be getting all steamed up about La Rochefoucauld. It's only a question of minutes before I'm going to be pretty darned good and sick of La Rochefoucauld, once and for all. La Rochefoucauld this and La Rochefoucauld that. Yes, well, let me tell you that if nobody had ever learned to quote, very few people would be in love with La Rochefoucauld. I bet you I don't know ten souls who read him without a middleman. People pick up those scholarly little essays that start off "Was it not that lovable old cynic, La Rochefoucauld, who said. . ." and then they go around claiming to know the master backwards. Pack of illiterates, that's all they are. All right, let them keep their La Rochefoucauld, and see if I care. I'll stick to La Fontaine. Only I'd be better company if I could quit thinking that La Fontaine married Alfred Lunt.

I don't know what I'm doing mucking about with a lot of French authors at this hour, anyway. First thing you know, I'll be reciting *Fleurs du Mal* to myself, and then I'll be little more good to anybody. And I'll stay off Verlaine too; he was always chasing Rimbauds. A person would be better off with La Rochefoucauld, even. Oh, damn La Rochefoucauld. The big Frog. I'll thank him to keep out of my head. What's La Rochefoucauld to me, or he to Hecuba? Why, I don't even know the man's first name, that's how close I ever was to *him*. What am I supposed to be, a hostess to La Rochefoucauld? That's what *he* thinks. Sez he. Well, he's only wasting his time, hanging around here. I can't help him. The only other thing I can remember his saying is that there is always something a little pleasing to us in the misfortunes of even our dearest friends. That cleans me all up with Monsieur La Rochefoucauld. *Maintenant ç'est fini, ça.*

Dearest friends. A sweet lot of dearest friends I've got. All of them lying in swinish stupors, while I'm practically up and about. All of them stretched sodden through these, the fairest hours of the day, when man should be at his most productive. Produce, produce, produce, for I tell you the night is coming. Carlyle said that. Yes, and a fine one *he* was, to go shooting off his face on production. *Oh*, Thomas Car *li*-yill, what I know about you-oo! No, that will be enough of that. I'm not going to start fretting about Carlyle, at this stage of the game. What did he ever do that was so great, besides founding a college for Indians? (That one ought to make him spin.) Let him keep his face out of this, if he knows what's good for him. I've got enough trouble with that lovable old cynic, La Rochefoucauld—him and the misfortunes of his dearest friends!

The first thing I've got to do is to get out and whip me up a complete new set of dearest friends; that's the first thing. Everything else can wait. And will somebody please kindly be so good as to inform me how I am ever going to meet up with any new people when my entire scheme of living is out of joint—when I'm the only living being awake while the rest of the world lies sleeping? I've got to get this thing adjusted. I must try to get back to sleep right now. I've got to conform to the rotten little standards of this sluggard civilization. People needn't feel that they have to change their ruinous habits and come my way. Oh, no, no; no, indeed. Not at all. I'll go theirs. If that isn't the woman of it for you! Always having to do what somebody else wants, like it or not. Never able to murmur a suggestion of her own.

And what suggestion has anyone to murmur as to how I am going to drift lightly back to slumber? Here I am, awake as high noon what with all this milling and pitching around with La Rochefoucauld. I really can't be expected to drop everything and start counting sheep, at my age. I hate sheep. Untender it may be in me, but all my life I've hated sheep. It amounts to a phobia, the way I hate them. I can tell the minute there's one in the room. They needn't think that I am going to lie here in the dark and count their unpleasant little faces for them; I wouldn't do it if I didn't fall asleep again until the middle of next August. Suppose they never get counted—what's the worst that can happen? If the number of imaginary sheep in this world remains a matter of guesswork, who is richer or poorer for it? No, sir; *I'm* not their scorekeeper. Let them count themselves, if they're so crazy mad after mathematics. Let them do their own dirty work. Coming around here, at this time of day, and asking me to count them! And not even *real* sheep, at that. Why, it's the most preposterous thing I ever heard in my life.

But there must be *something* I could count. Let's see. No, I already know by heart how many fingers I have. I could count my bills, I suppose. I could count the things I didn't do yesterday that I should have done. I could count the things I should do today that I'm not going to do. I'm never going to accomplish anything; that's perfectly clear to me. I'm never going to be famous. My name will never be writ large on the roster of Those Who Do Things. I don't do anything. Not one single thing. I used to bite my nails, but I don't even do that anymore. I don't amount to the powder to blow me to hell. I've turned out to be nothing but a bit of flotsam. Flotsam and leave 'em—that's me from now on. Oh, it's all terrible.

Well. This way lies galloping melancholia. Maybe it's because this is the zero hour. This is the time the swooning soul hangs pendant and vertiginous between the new day and the old, nor dares confront the one or summon back the other. This is the time when all things, known and hidden, are iron to weight the spirit; when all ways, traveled or virgin, fall away from the stumbling feet, when all before the straining eyes is black. Blackness now, everywhere is blackness. This is the time of abomination, the dreadful hour of the victorious dark. For it is always darkest—Was it not that lovable old cynic, La Rouchefoucauld, who said it is always darkest before the deluge?

There. Now you see, don't you? Here we are again, practically back where we started. La Rochefoucauld, we are here. Ah, come on, son—how about your going your way and letting me go mine? I've got my work cut out for me right here; I've got all this sleeping to do. Think how I am going to look by daylight if this keeps up. I'll be a seamy sight for all those rested, clear-eyed, fresh-faced dearest friends of mine—the rats! My *dear*, whatever have you been doing; I thought you were so good lately. Oh, I was helling around with La Rochefoucauld till all hours; we couldn't stop laughing about your misfortunes. No, this is getting too thick, really. It isn't right to have this happen to a person, just because she went to bed at ten o'clock once in her life. Honest, I won't ever do it again. I'll go straight, after this. I'll never go to bed again, if I can only sleep now. If I can tear my mind away from a certain French cynic, *circa* 1650, and slip into lovely oblivion. 1650. I better look as if I'd been awake since then.

How do people go to sleep? I'm afraid I've lost the knack. I might try busting myself smartly over the temple with the night-light. I might repeat to myself, slowly and soothingly, a list of quotations beautiful from minds profound; if I can remember any of the damn things. That might do it. And it ought effectually to bar that visiting foreigner that's been hanging around ever since twenty minutes past four. Yes, that's what I'll do. Only wait till I turn the pillow; it feels as if La Rochefoucauld had crawled inside the slip.

Now let's see—where shall we start? Why—er—let's see. Oh, yes, I know one. This above all, to thine own self be true and it must follow, as the night the day, thou canst not then be false to any man. Now they're off. And once they get started, they ought to come like hot cakes. Let's see. Ah, what avail the sceptered race and what the form divine, when every virtue, every grace, Rose Aylmer, all were thine. Let's see. They also serve who only stand and wait. If Winter comes, can Spring be far behind? Lilies that fester smell far worse than weeds. Silent upon a peak in Darien. Mrs. Porter and her daughter wash their feet in soda-water. And Agatha's Arth is a hug-the-hearth, but my true love is false. Why did you die when lambs were cropping, you should have died when apples were dropping. Shall be together, breathe and ride, so one day more am I deified, who knows but the world will end tonight. And he shall hear the stroke of eight and not the stroke of nine. They are not long, the weeping and the laughter; love and desire and hate I think will have no portion in us after we pass the gate. But none, I think, do there embrace. I think that I shall never see a poem lovely as a tree. I think I will not hang myself today. Ay tank Ay go home now.

Let's see. Solitude is the safeguard of mediocrity and the stern companion of genius. Consistency is the hob-goblin of little minds. Something is emotion remembered in tranquillity. A cynic is one who knows the price of everything and the value of nothing. That lovable old cynic is one who—oops, there's King Charles's head again. I've got to watch myself. Let's see. Circumstantial evidence is a trout in the milk. Any stigma will do to beat a dogma. If you would learn what God thinks about money, you have only to look at those to whom He has given it. If nobody had ever learned to read, very few people—

All right. That fixes it. I throw in the towel right now. I know when I'm licked. There'll be no more of this nonsense; I'm going to turn on the light and read my head off. Till the next ten o'clock, if I feel like it. And what does La Rochefoucauld want to make of that? Oh, he *will*, eh? Yes, he will! He and who else? La Rochefoucauld and *what* very few people?

Dorothy Parker

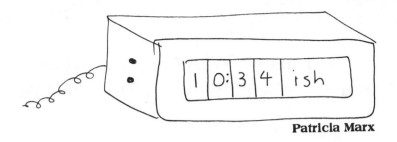

Patricia Marx

Too Busy to Fall in Love?

The most ridiculous thing I ever heard
was someone saying they were "too busy to fall in love."
Look, the busier you are,
the more imperative it is to fall in love.
Love is necessary to balance your perception of Time.
When you have too much to do,
time goes by so fast.
Yet when you are in love,
the time between seeing your beloved goes so slow.
Love is the imbalance that balances Time.

Flash Rosenberg

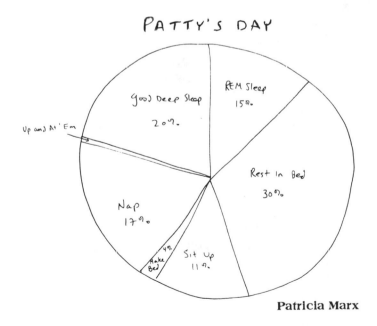

PATTY'S DAY

Patricia Marx

For Those Who Suffer from Chronic Mismanagement of Their Own Time

Leave work one half hour early.
Think of all you could be doing to fill up
    this small treasure of open time.
On a large sheet of paper
make a list of every one of those things you know
    you ought to be doing
or rather, make a chart.
Write upside down, along the edges and in corners.
Draw detailed diagrams with step by step instructions.
Include intricate illustration, underlining,
    and exclamation points!
Don't stop
    until every square inch of space is full.
Make it as demanding, as imposing
    as impossible as you like.

Make it as demanding,
    and imposing
    and impossible as your life.
Read it over and take it all in.
Next, crease the chart evenly into a fold
    along one edge.
Turn it over and fold again.
Continue until you have pleated the entire surface
    into a paper fan.
All the words and diagrams will make
    interesting designs along the edges and will be
    completely illegible.
Fan in hand,
stretch out full length in a comfortable spot.
Gently fan yourself to sleep.

Becky Birtha

Equal Time

Youknow, recently one of our most distinguished Americans, Clare Boothe Luce, had this to say about the coming vote [on aid to the Contras]. "...My mind goes back to a similar moment in our history—back to the first years after Cuba had fallen to Fidel. One day during those years, I had lunch at the White House with a man I had known since he was a boy—John F. Kennedy. 'Mr. President,' I said, 'no matter how exalted or great a man may be, history will have time to give him no more than one sentence. George Washington—he founded our country. Abraham Lincoln—he freed the slaves and preserved the union.'"

—Ronald Reagan
(*address to the nation, March 16, 1986*)

William Henry Harrison: He was the first occupant of the White House to eat with a knife and fork.

Millard Fillmore: He had his own likeness secretly engraved in the folds of Miss Liberty's dress on the 1851 Silver Dollar.

Franklin Pierce: He earned the sobriquets Old Tongue-in-Groove and The Gabardine Gangplank.

Ulysses S. Grant: He translated the words to "The Star-Spangled Banner" into thirteen different languages, including mirror writing.

Benjamin Harrison: He predicted the birth of the Dionne Quintuplets over forty years before it happened.

William McKinley: He was his own grandfather.

Warren G. Harding: He campaigned on a bicycle carved from a single giant bar of soup.

Calvin Coolidge: He coined the catchphrase of the era—"Do you simply want a cigarette or do you want a Murad?"

Herbert Hoover: He reorganized the National Christmas Card Cemetery.

Gerald Ford: He had the idea for *Shampoo* long before the movie came out.

Ronald Reagan: He popularized the political theories of Clare Boothe Luce.

Veronica Geng

Nikki Gosch

Dianne Reum

My Life: A Series of Privately Funded Performance-Art Pieces

Birth

As the piece opens, another performance artist, "Mom" (an affiliate of my private funding source) waits onstage, consuming tuna-noodle casseroles. Eventually, she leaves the initial performance site—a single-family Cape Cod decorated with amoeboid sofas, Herman Miller coconut chairs, boomerang-print linoleum, and semi-shag carpeting—for a second site, a hospital. There she is joined by a sterile-clad self-realized figure of authority ("Sidney Jaffe, M.D.") who commands her to "push," and then externalizes through language and gesture his desire to return to the back nine. This tableau makes allusion to the deadening, depersonalizing, postwar "good life." "Mom" continues "pushing," and at last I enter—nude. I do this in a manner that confronts yet at the same time steers clear of all obscenity statutes.

Coming home extremely late because I was making snow angels and forgot to stop

Again, an ensemble piece. But unlike "Birth," which explores the universal codes of pleasure and vulnerability, "Coming Home Extremely Late" is a manifesto about rage—not mine but that of the protonuclear family. The cast includes "Mom," "David," "Debra," "Fluffy," and my private funding source. In "Coming Home," I become Object, rather than Subject.

The piece is also a metaperformance; the more sophisticated members of the audience will realize that I am "coming home extremely late" because of *another* performance: "Snow Angels," an earlier, gestural work in which, clothed in a cherry-red Michelin Man-style snowsuit, I lower myself into a snowbank and wave my arms up and down, leaving a winged-creature-like impression upon the frozen palimpsest. Owing to my methodology, I am better at it than anyone on the block. Note the megatextual references to Heaven, Superior Being-as-girl-child, snow-as-inviolable-purity, and time-as-irrelevancy. "Coming Home Extremely Late" concludes with a choral declaration from the entire cast (except for my private funding source, who has turned to reading the sports section), titled "You Are Grounded For a Month, Young Lady."

I go through a gangly period

A sustained dramatic piece, lasting three to five years, depending on how extensively the performer pursues the orthodontia theme. Besides me, the cast includes the entire student population of Byron Junior High School, Shaker Heights, Ohio—especially the boys. In the course of "Gangly Period," I grow large in some ways, small in others, and, ironically, they are all the wrong ways. I receive weird haircuts. Through "crabby" behavior (mostly directed at my private funding source), my noncontextual stage image projects the unspeakable fear that I am not "popular." In a surreal trope midway through the performance, I vocalize to a small section of the cast ("Ellen Fisher," "Sally Webb," and "Heather Siegel") my lack of knowledge about simple sexual practices.

Throughout the piece, much commentary about time: how long it is, why certain things seem to take forever, why I have to be the absolutely last girl in the entire seventh grade to get Courrèges boots.

Finding Myself

This piece is a burlesque—a comic four-year-long high art/low art exploration. As "Finding Myself" opens, I am on-site—a paradigmatic bourgeois college campus. After performing the symbiotic ritual of "meeting my roommates" and dialoguing about whether boyfriends can stay overnight in our room, I reject the outmoded, parasitic escape route of majoring in English, and instead dare to enroll in a class called "Low Energy Living," in which I reject the outmoded, parasitic escape route of reading the class material and instead build a miniature solar-powered seawater-desalinization plant. I then confront Amerika's greedy soulless-ness by enrolling in a class called "Future Worlds," walking around in a space suit of my own design, doing a discursive/nonlinear monologue on Buckminster Fuller and futurism.

Toward the end of "Finding Myself," I skip all my "classes"—spatially as well as temporally—and move into an alternative environment to examine my "issues." At this point, my private funding source actually appears in the piece and, in a witty cameo, threatens to withdraw my grant. Much implosive controversy. To close the performance, I sit on an avocado-green beanbag chair and simulate "applying to graduate school."

I get married and shortly thereafter take a pounding in the real estate market

A bifurcated work. First, another performance artist, "Peter," dialogues with me about the explicit, symbolic, and functional presentations of human synchronism. We then plan and execute a suburban country-club wedding (again, with assistance from my private funding source). Making a conceptual critique of materialism, I "register" for Royal Copenhagen china, Baccarat crystal, and Kirk Stieff sterling. Syllabic chants, fragments of unintelligible words like the screeches of caged wild birds gone mad—this megatonality erupts when I confront my private funding source about seating certain little-liked relatives. At the work's interactive climax, "Peter" and I explode the audience/performer dialectic and invite the audience to join as we "perform the ceremony."

The second part of the piece—a six-month-long open-ended manifesto on the specificity of place—culminates with "Peter" and me purchasing a four-and-a-half-room cooperative apartment with a good address in Manhattan. Conran's furniture, Krups appliances, task-specific gadgets (apple corers, pasta makers, shrimp de-veiners), and other symbol-laden icons are arranged on-site. Curtain goes down on the performers facing each other on a sofa, holding a *Times* real-estate section between them, doing performative discourse lamenting that they have "purchased the apartment at the peak of the market."

The series will continue pending refinancing.

Susan Orlean

Off-Ramp

I used to speak the language of the patriarchy.

Rick, my stepfather, taught me Latin names for all the bones in his right foot. When I helped my first boyfriend with his high-school homework, he insisted I do it in baby talk.

And then there was Lyle. He came into the Carl's Jr. that Rick and my mom run near Flagstaff, Arizona, one day in late August. All summer we fed tourists after they were Grand Canyoned out. Hundreds—*thousands*— of exhausted, screaming kids and their zombified parents. I was nineteen. Lyle was sitting alone that afternoon, staring at me while I loaded French-fry bags.

"Tell that creep he's got to give up his table," Rick said. "He's been there fifteen minutes."

I went over to where Lyle was lounging. "My stepdad thinks it's impolite to digest your food," I told him.

Lyle looked deep into my eyes. "Doreen," he said, reading my nameplate. "I have news for you, Doreen. You are not who you think you are. You are not a fast-food server—you are an inspiration from the divine. You have made me want to create again."

"I have?" I said. "Are you an artist?"

"I could be," he said, "if you would be my muse." He paused and played with his straw. "Do you know what a muse is?" I shook my head. "A muse is a woman who makes it possible for a guy to carry out his life's work. But muses don't have names like Doreen."

He stood up and left. I ran after him.

"Then who am I?" I asked in the parking lot.

"Henceforth," he said, "you shall be Rawnee." He spelled it in the dust on his van.

I'd never been with anyone who lived for his art before. The people I knew all picked up after themselves. But Lyle couldn't function without me. And I thought I was discovering capabilities in myself I hadn't known were there, like paying bills.

We went through my junior-college savings fund in two weeks.

One night Lyle drove off without saying anything. I was terrified that he wouldn't come back, that he'd find another muse. At 3 a.m. he returned, carrying a huge cardboard box. "All the really creative people have to be subsidized," he explained. He knifed open the carton. Clothing labels spilled out onto the shag carpeting of the tiny house we were renting. "You and me are about to get a little grant from Mack Ropington," he said.

It was at the height of the Western-wear craze, and everyone was splurging on Ropington's designer clothes and furnishings. I knew that what we were about to do was wrong and, worse, that I could end up in jail.

"Do you think what *Ropington's* doing is right?" Lyle asked. "Making people think they're cowboys because they're wearing his hundred-dollar jeans or sleeping under his five-hundred dollar horse blankets?"

"No, but—"

"I thought you loved me," Lyle said.

So, the next day I got up before dawn and drove out into the Verde Valley. I met up with my contact on a dirt road full of potholes. I paid him for his trunkful of men's cotton briefs—they were the kind you'd buy at K-mart. Then I sat in my car and sewed in the tags. When I finished, it was 8 a.m., time to drive over to the Sedona off-ramp and set up shop. That day I cleared $169.52.

I was always selling something different. Sometimes it was ties, sometimes shirts, sometimes pillowcases, pot holders, or mittens. Whatever my supplier could get—and I never asked how. People would stop their cars to buy it as long as it said Ropington.

My new career had its downside, too. I often had to change locations to avoid getting caught. And later, when the recession hit, the tourists started keeping their disposable income for vacation essentials such as motel childcare.

Lyle, however, was *always* having a hard time. "How can I create art when the world's so messed up?" he said one night. I was sitting on the bed, sewing labels into imitation-leather aprons. "I should be out making a difference," he said. "I should go leave tire tracks on the front lawn of the White House to let them know what I think of their energy policies."

"Lyle," I said, "you have to make things better where you can. And no improvement is too small."

He thought about this. "You're right, Rawnee," he said. "While you're doing that, take off your clothes."

"Lyle," I said, "I'm *working*." But I never could refuse him.

"The world's a better place already," he said.

Astra says that men have separated themselves from nature, and that's why in these last few years of this millennium Lyle can't create.

I was going to goddess therapy. I saw the ad for it in our newspaper. "Find the Power of Inspiration Within—Let the Muse Speak to *You*," it said. I was sure this was what I needed to help Lyle.

We met every Tuesday evening at the public library, because it was over the strongest power vortex in our town. Unfortunately, the library closed that spring for lack of funding. We then got together at Denny's on 89, which is on top of the second-strongest power vortex.

"This Astra is taking advantage of you," Lyle said. "She is leading you on, Rawnee, when she says that you can create art. Let me tell you, not everyone can create art. Even if you're an artist, it doesn't mean you can create art."

"Astra says that if you connect with the feminine you will achieve wholeness, and then you will create."

"Rawnee," he said, "the kind of wholeness *I* need to create art is matched pairs of socks in my drawer, and a refrigerator full of food. You've been neglecting things around here, especially me."

Astra felt I had it in me to perform my own ritual. I was nervous. The rituals that the other women had created were *so* impressive! One sat for three days in our local river. Another shaved her head and ate mud.

"Stop thinking and it will come to you," Astra said.

It was while I was selling at the Canyon de Chelly on-ramp that I had a revelation about what form my ritual must take. I phoned all the wo-men and invited them over to our house. Lyle was furious when I made him leave.

"I'm interested in getting in touch with my primordial wo-maness-ness," I announced. It was a suffocatingly hot July night. "So I'm going to turn off the air-conditioner."

We sweltered together for an hour, and then Astra spoke. "I don't mean to be hierarchical or anything," she said to me, "but I think you can do better."

September 10th was a particularly bad day for me. My 5 a.m. contact could only get abalone shells. It took me forever to paste the Ropington tags into them. Then drivers just slowed down at the Moenkopi off-ramp and eyed me suspiciously. They didn't stop.

By noon I'd developed a halfway decent sales pitch. "Mack Ropington says the era of the West he's gaining the most inspiration from these days is when it was all underwater," I'd say.

Not one sale.

Early that afternoon, a colleague set up beside me. I recognized him from various junctions and cloverleafs where he'd always dressed in old miner's gear. Now, he was wearing mirror shades, a poncho, and braids.

My heart sank when he propped up a dozen paintings on velvet. Sure enough, a man in an Infiniti screeched to a stop. He pointed to a picture of a chief offering a scalp to a naked squaw. "I really go for the Native American philosophy of life," the Infiniti man said.

"That's five per cent off the asking price for not calling us Indians," my competition said.

I got home around nine. All I wanted was to go straight to bed. When I opened the door, I didn't recognize my home. The furniture had been totally rearranged. And a woman *I'd* never seen before was draping herself on the couch I'd purchased.

"Who are you?" I demanded.

"Calm down," she said. "Nothing happened. Lyle and I are exploring the spiritual side of our relationship."

Lyle strolled into the room. He didn't say as much as hello to me.

"What's going on?" I said.

"Rawnee," he said, "meet Tawnee."

"Lyle," she whined, "I think it's time we advanced to touching. I'm getting achy in my shoulders from all the tension in the air."

He looked at me and sighed. "It's damn hard to be an artist in this house. On top of all *your* questions, now I have to give *her* a *massage*."

At that, I started packing my things.

When Lyle saw I was serious about leaving, he blocked the front door. "Rawnee," he said. "You can't abandon me. You know how much you mean to me. You are the air that gives me life, the water that sustains me—"

"And the earth you walk all over," I said.

I needed a ritual that would transform my hurt into a mighty but sensitive sword. I drove high into the mesas with Astra and the others. We left our vehicles behind and climbed up a rock and into a cave. There we swept aside the used condoms and beer bottles.

"Let the wind and sky speak to you," Astra told me.

I tried.

"What are they saying?"

"I'm not sure," I said.

"You're thinking again," she said.

"Don't think. Deep within you is the power to understand."

I listened again. This time I heard their voices.

"Forget that jerk," the voices said.

I have left Rawnee behind, and I have no more need of Mack Ropington's name. I am Superba now, and I have my own resonant image.

Two cars pull up to my stand. "Hey, that's you, isn't it?" The man in the white Bronco says. He casts his eyes on my wares: photos of me printed on T-shirts. "I'll take three of the ones with you topless."

The other driver gets out of his Hyundai. "Excuse me," he says. "Did I hear you say 'topless'? This is not a T-shirt with a photo on it of a topless woman. This is a T-shirt with a photo on it of a woman who has chosen to bare her breasts." This man turns to me. "I'm Coe," he says. "I'm white, I'm male, I'm heterosexual, and I'm sorry."

"I'm Superba," I tell him. "And I need to exorcise some submission forces arising in me upon meeting a man after being single for three months. I need to do this in a context in which I still honor my own power. So this is how it's going to be—you will pick a restaurant, drive us there, and pay for dinner."

We are travelling along a winding mountain road. He relates the story of his quest to attain a genuine PMS state. His Hyundai begins to sputter. Moments later, we are out of gas.

Coe bursts into tears. "This is a metaphor for how the patriarchy's breaking down and me with it!" He clutches me and sobs. "Show me the way, Superba."

"Well," I say, "one of the first things I do when I get in a car is look at the gas gauge."

"You're a woman warrior!" he cries. He straightens up. "I've been reading Carl Jung. He says a man is nothing until he meets his anima. Please be my feminine principle and help me become whole again."

I pull him to me and kiss him. "Wow," he says. "The way you're in charge of your sexuality is devastating to my male ego. But it's the only chance our planet has."

I kiss him again. Together we acknowledge the presence of nature. Snow is falling. The road is dark, and it doesn't appear likely that automobiles will pass by.

"What do we do now?" he asks.

"One of us must seek out a twenty-four-hour filling station and return with some gas."

"I lost my intuitive powers when my Fathers colonized your sex," he says. "We'll be doomed if *I* try to find one."

"You're right," I say. "You must stay here." I gather my purse, put on my jacket, and look over at Coe. He is trembling; there are holes in his sweater. The sight of him expressing his true male helplessness summons forth my inner voices. As Astra has taught me, I listen to them. "Remove your own parka and tuck it around him," the voices say.

I obey, then open the car door and step out. "You're my kind of goddess," he calls out from the inside. "Hurry back."

The snow crunches under my sneakers. I am shivering, but that will pass. For I am the strong one.

Polly Frost

activism

It was not easy driving with an
animal rights activist.

Real Life Drama

(Darkened stage. Sound of a Greyhound bus fading into the distance. Spotlight up on lone lesbian activist, suitcase in hand. She waves goodbye to the departing bus, saying:)

Lesbian: Thanks, Mr. Busdriver! Wow. I finally made it to Americaville, U.S.A.—home of the 9th Annual Womyn's Workshop Festival. What a quaint, lower-middle class setting—the perfect place for me to pass out my leaflets on radical feminist chakra awareness in the workplace. First, though, I think I'll go across the street and get a sandwich. Golly. I just can't wait to begin to effect social change!

(Lights down. Suddenly, a screech of heavy tires is heard, then a thud. Lights come up on the original American Gothic couple, sitting on the porch of their dilapidated house, up the hill from the corner where the lesbian stood. Pa is snoozing in his rocker; Ma puts down her knitting and looks out, in the direction of the noise.)

Ma: Hey, Pa.

Pa: Yeah, Ma?

Ma: There's a big ol' lesbian lying in the middle of the road.

Pa: I believe I heard that one before, Ma.

Ma: This ain't no joke, Pa. A cement truck just come outta nowhere and knocked that lesbian down.

Pa: How you know she's a lesbian, Ma?

Ma: Bowl haircut. Social change leaflets. Teeny hatchet hangin' off'n her left ear. A woman knows these things, Pa.

Pa: She ain't one of them bachelor gals in the overalls who goes around wearing them "Vegetarians Against Hormel" buttons?

Ma: The same. *(Pause. Ma goes back to her knitting. Pa, now fully awake, seems troubled.)*

Pa: Hey, Ma.

Ma: Yeah, Pa?

Pa: I feel kinda bad sittin' here on the porch in total comfort, while the lesbian's lyin' down there all alone. Why, even that cement truck went off and left her. Maybe I ought to throw myself onto the median next to the lesbian.

Ma: Now, Pa. Don't you go actin' like one of them guilt-crazed liberals. I swear, ever since the bank done took away our farm, you just ain't been yourself.

Pa: *(Pa's hands go to either side of his head; his eyes open wide; he begins to rock back and forth agitatedly.)* The bank, Ma! The bank!

Ma: Oh, lord—I knew I shouldn't have brought that up again...

Pa: Lookee here, Ma—the bank owned our farm, right?

Ma: Right, Pa.

Pa: And the bank told us what to do, right?

Ma: Right, Pa.

Pa: And the bank probably owns that cement company, right?

Ma: Probably, Pa. But—

Pa: You know, Ma, I'm beginnin' to see a pattern here... *(Suddenly rises and declaims.)* "It is organized violence on top which creates individual violence at the bottom." That's Emma Goldman, Ma.

Ma: Pa, you're not feelin' well. Let me make you some nice tea—

Pa: *(Throws down his cane in exhilaration.)* Hallelujah, Ma! I done had me a Revelation! The same societal forces what took our farm done knocked that Lesbian down. We've all been trampled under the wheels of a male-dominated, heterosexist, white supremacist, imperialistic military-industrial complex, writhing in the insidious throes of advanced post-capitalist decline. Glory be, Ma—I'm a' speakin' in tongues!

Ma: Why don't we just help the poor li'l gal up, Pa?

Pa: *(Begins to march around the porch, chanting.)* Gay/Straight; Black/White—Together We Struggle; Together We Fight! We gotta form coalitions with other oppressed groups, Ma. ¡La Lucha Continua!

Ma: Now you listen here, Pa. Either you start talkin' sense, or I'm leaving you!

Pa: I think you mean, Ma, that "A Woman without a man is like a fish without a bicycle." Oh praise Jesus! He done put the holy words of Gloria Steinem into my mouth!

Ma: Pa! Don't you know the Russians *want* you to talk like that?

Pa: Au contraire, Ma. We gotta celebrate our differences! That lesbian down yonder is making a, what you call, "non-violent protest." She's sayin' that, although we may be knocked down and left for dead by the cement truck of History, there is still hope if we but have the courage to lie there and stand for something! She's—*(Ma is peering out at the intersection.)*

Ma: Uh, Pa, darlin'?

Pa: Yeah, Comrade Ma?

Ma: She ain't there no more.

Pa: How's that?

Ma: The lesbian done got up by herself and limped away. *(Long pause, during which Pa sits back in his rocker. He looks shaken and hurt. Finally, he regroups.)*

Pa: Oh well. She probably has other towns to go to; other cement trucks to meet. Gotta spread the word, I reckon.

Ma: I reckon. *(Pause.)*

Pa: You know, Ma, maybe we should do something nice for the lesbian. Sort of say, "Thanks for being there."

Ma: Like what, Pa?

Pa: Hold one of them there "Gay Pride" marches.

Ma: I give up. Go ahead, Pa, if it'll make you happy.

Pa: Hot diggity! I'm gonna telephone the boys down at the V.W.F. to help me get the balloons all blowed up.

Ma: Maybe if you asked real polite, Pa, I'd sew you some nice "gay 'n proud" banners.

Pa: And I bet we could use that cement truck for a float!

Ma: What?—Work within the System for social change?! Are you crazy, Pa? This has got to be total Revolution or nuthin'! . . . *(They continue fomenting peaceably, rocking back and forth, as the lights fade.)*

Susie Day

Cath Jackson

Alison Bechdel

My Friend Is Giving Me a
Mid-life Crisis

It's obvious to me that the books and magazine articles about middle age have left out a few chapters. After reading several books about the mid-life crisis and the psychological impact of middle age, I have come to the conclusion that either the psychologists or the editors or maybe both are under 30 and don't really understand what the important changes are in middle age and how difficult it is to channel talents that took 20 years to develop and polish.

First the experts write volumes about the sex lives of mature adults. Who are we kidding? By the time you reach middle-age, you have either learned how to live with sex or you have learned how to live without sex. If you haven't found the sexual revolution by the time you're 40, you probably wouldn't want to enlist anyway.

Then there's all that old hygiene class stuff, the physical changes like the law of gravity and its effects on the body. Then one has to deal with the dilemma of gray hair, or no hair, and wrinkles. It's too bad permanent press hasn't caught up with human evolution. Personal choice leaves the middle-aged adult with two options: let it be or fight it with gusto.

What the books about middle-age leave out is what to do with the talents that 20 or so years of parenthood instilled. Remember when the only words your child knew were "Can I have an advance in my allowance?" and "Mom, you're embarrassing me." Parents have adapted to the first phrase by giving generous gifts and co-signing loans. But who do you embarrass when the kids aren't there?

I'm sure by now all the psychologists are sitting on the edges of their chairs and so I will attempt to explain this psychological phenomenon by presenting a case history.

Last Sunday my friend, Eleanor, and I went to a symphony concert in the park. We were very impressive. We took a picnic of champagne, pate, silver, linen and even the heirloom candlesticks.

We didn't want to be ostentatious so we left the butler at home and didn't light the candles.

As the psychologists would say, we were "socially appropriate." We applauded in all the right places and yelled "encore" at the end of the concert.

Our children would have been so proud. Nothing lasts forever, though.

As we started to leave, Eleanor spotted the garbage can. Aluminum cans sparkled in the summer sunset and Eleanor was off on her special mission. You see, Eleanor is the queen of recycling in our community.

She was very polite and asked the police officer on duty for permission to go through the garbage. He gave her the only answer a cop who has spent six hours patrolling a crowd on a hot July day in the park could give, "Knock yourself out lady, it's all yours."

He even advised the sanitation crew to come back later because that can had Eleanor's name on it.

I was a little squeamish about the whole project, but Eleanor assured me that since it was fresh, it was "clean garbage."

We managed to salvage about four pounds from the first can. By the time we got to the third can, Eleanor was on a roll. Soon a truck pulled up and a jocular man stepped out and walked over to us.

"I'm Nick and I own the Busy Bee Cafe downtown. I did the catering today. If you two ladies will stop by tomorrow, I'll see that you get lunch."

Eleanor tried to explain that she didn't need a meal, she just liked to recycle cans.

Nick seemed to really admire her pride—he was a gentleman through and through.

"Don't worry lady, after you eat lunch, you can have all the cans at the place. In fact, from now on, I'll save all my cans for you."

Eleanor was so thrilled about getting a restaurant full of cans to recycle, she didn't even comprehend that Nick thought she needed a good solid meal. She thanked him so profusely for the cans that he was becoming convinced she was a bag lady.

When Nick left, I said, "Eleanor, I want your daughter's telephone number."

"Whatever for?" queried Eleanor.

"I need to talk to somebody who understands," I replied.

Brenda Lawlor

'Oh yes, we're very into recycling.
I use all Bob's old underpants
as dishcloths'

Ros Asquith

Title Equality—A New Approach

I filled out a form at my dentist's office the other day. It was your basic form with a choice of three boxes to check for your appropriate title. Like this:

❏ Mr
❏ Mrs _____
❏ Miss

We've all filled out these forms. We simply take it all in our stride and fill them out like this:

❏ ~~Mr~~
❏ ~~Mrs~~ _____ *Ms. Sally Jones*
❏ ~~Miss~~

It's just a little thing we do in hopes that some day society will catch onto the fact that women cannot be so easily categorized. It's just a little thing that we hope will lead to bigger things, like equal pay, reproductive freedom and safety from brutality and rape. It's just a little thing that I've been doing for twenty years and I'm beginning to wonder if it will ever catch on.

Society has not caught on to the philosophy behind the Ms title. Oh, sure, the term Ms is included on some forms. The forms look like this:

❏ Mr
❏ Mrs _____
❏ Miss
❏ Ms

But the idea was for women to be less categorized, not more. Men, they exist. They are men. That's all we need to know. For women, existing is not enough. Women are still being asked to label themselves before we will accept their names on a form. Okay, so we've recognized that this is unfair. We've said, "We will use a title equal to the male formal title." And we have been using it for twenty years and it hasn't worked. If it had worked, the staff at my dentist's office wouldn't still be calling me Mrs. Jones.

However, I have not given up on the idea that title equality might lead to more important equalities for women. Perhaps we have just gone about obtaining equal titles in the wrong way. Maybe instead of changing female titles to correspond to male titles, we should be encouraging men to use titles that reveal something about themselves. I suppose the masculine equivalent to the term Ms would be Mr, but Mr just doesn't make the same statement as Ms. It's so trite and anonymous. It just won't do for the man who wants to make a statement about his individuality. For the man whose aura fairly shouts, "My marital status is none of your business!" how about the title "Mys," as in mystery. Mys Robert Jones. Of course, in oral conversation you couldn't tell the difference between "Ms" and "Mys," Now that's equality.

Perhaps we should also encourage men (if they are so inclined) to choose a title that allows them to proclaim their state of marital bliss. For the man who is proud to be married and wants the world to know, what else, "Mrd." Mrd Robert Jones. Then obviously the next necessary title would be "Unmrd." Unmrd Robert Jones or just plain Unmrd Jones. With just these basic changes, the form at the dentist's office would look like this:

❑ Mys

❑ Ms   _____

❑ Mrd

❑ Mrs

❑ Unmrd

❑ Miss

But why stop there? Why should men be limited to choosing only titles that correspond to traditional female titles? How about:

Mu	Unable to commit
Mm	Monogamist
Mcs	Cooks a mean spaghetti sauce
Mnd	Never changed a dirty diaper
M$	Makes over $500,000 a year
Mp	Likes pets
Mcd	Celibate after messy divorce
M2w	Currently dating two women
Mlmr	Looking for Miss Right
Mlmsr	Looking for Ms Right
Mv	Have had a vasectomy
Mo	Over thirty and living with parents

The possibilities are endless. Go ahead, fellas, make up your very own title, or if you don't like to be so expressive (especially on routine forms), you could still use Mr. But I can just hear the form checker say, "Hmmm, one of those. He's not telling his marital status. He's probably a radical masculinist." You might as well pick a title that's really you. I'm sure that society could come up with about a dozen titles to be included on all routine forms. Of course, it would require a lot more paper and ink. A new government agency would probably have to be set up, but what the heck, this is vital information for the women of the nineties. Remember what's good for the goose is good for the gander. Is that a single gander or a gander that's involved with someone?

Sherry Wallace

MRS & MR
DAR & DARS
STONE

Martha Campbell

Marian Henley

Kathryn LeMieux

Roberta Gregory

☺ We bring you— live, from the scene of the tragedy..... ☹

cont. →

282

Angela Bocage

Don't Touch that Remote!

I confess. I like T.V. commercials. A creative, over-active brain like mine has a field day with them—especially when the sound is off. You just gotta know how to improve 'em.

One of my favorites is a gourmet coffee commercial. Two women are sitting together on a boat, sipping their coffee, enjoying the sunrise, professing their devout friendship for each other.

Just when you think it's going to get interesting, one of them says, "Should we wake the guys?"—a line which assures us, in case anyone was getting nervous, that these women are straight.

In her best conspiratorial tone, the other says, "No, let's keep this all to ourselves".

"Ha, ha. Those girls are feisty," the viewers chuckle, "though not dangerous to the moral fiber of this great nation."

Now let's hit the mute button and open up *a lot* more possibilities. Okay, the women (we'll call them Krista and Jenny) are still on the boat, still watching the sunrise, but...

Krista: A perfect morning! A brilliant sunrise, a cup of General Thrills Swiss Mocha®, and a good friend. What more could one ask for?

Jenny: Now that you mention it.... I have an incredible crush on you and want to make passionate love right here, right now on the deck of this boat.

Krista: Think we should wake the guys?

Jenny: No. I want this moment all to ourselves. Besides, I threw them both overboard last night.

Krista: Oh, so *that's* what that splashing was all about. Well, darling, I'm all yours. Come give me a long, deep kiss.

Voice Over. General Thrills International Coffees. Celebrate the moments of your life.

Now, sometimes, turning off the sound and making up new words doesn't help a bit. One such case in point is a truly offensive commercial for Mazda's latest truck, The Navajo. Not surprisingly, members of the Navajo community are ticked off about the name of this vehicle. To name *any* automobile—much less an off-road vehicle that tears up the fragile ecoscape—after the Navajo people is a disgrace.

But wait. It gets worse. You see, the commercial is one of those high-tech, quick shots types: Picture of the southwest desert. Click! Off-road vehicle zips up the road. Switch shots. A kiva, with a ladder emerging. Back to the truck: a close-in shot of a brawny Caucasian male at the wheel. Flash! A petroglyph etched on a canyon wall. Cut to brawny driver who whips vehicle past sunset, then brakes with testosterone-filled precision. He jumps from vehicle, strides toward stereotype of female Native American. Flash! Progressive-minded viewers at home throw up.

There are a lot of reasons to hate this commercial. For starters, it's loaded with "macho man conquers nature and natives" garbage. But I'd like to focus on the kivas, petroglyphs and canyons. For the Navajo people, these are spiritual images and places. They are what mainstream America calls "religious imagery." Odd, isn't it, that a car company would use religion to sell its products. Can you imagine them doing that with Christian imagery? Probably not. But I can...

Therefore, I present to you the ultimate high-powered, off-road vehicle...The Presbyterian!

Setting: The Holy Land. (Where else?) A bright star rises in the east.

Action: Three weary but wise men trudge towards Bethlehem. Appearing out of nowhere, a flashy, aggressive vehicle zooms past them. It's the Presbyterian! Leaving the wise men choking in the dust, the camera cuts to the tan guy in the driver's seat. He flashes us a perfect white-toothed smile.

Click! The Presbyterian zips by a crowd gathered around a mount. As one, all heads turn away from Jesus to watch instead the truly splendid awe of this miraculous automotive machine.

Flash! The Presbyterian speeds past a group of mourners. Even before Jesus can approach the casket, Lazarus rises from the dead, driven by the desire to catch a brief glimpse of the Presbyterian as it tears by. The camera cuts to the driver who lowers his shades, throwing us a self-assured, manly look.

Flash! Time for real action: Shifting into four-wheel drive, the driver puts the pedal to the metal and the Presbyterian rips up a rugged hill. Three crosses appear in the distance. It's Calvary!

Boom! The driver brings the vehicle to a screeching halt, leaps out of his seat. As he strides towards the crosses, Mary Magdalene breaks out of the crowd, and runs towards him, arms open wide.

Voice Over. The Presbyterian: With off-road power like this—who needs a higher power?

Ellen Orleans

Marian Henley

Mugged

for Marilyn Silberglied

It wasn't enough with the pogroms, the poverty, the cold, the hunger, with everything in my life I've ever been through, you'd think in my old age I could enjoy a little peace and quiet, but no, that would be too good for me. Somewhere it must be written that Esther Silberglied hasn't suffered enough.

Once a month I take the D train from the Bronx into Manhattan to get my hair done, at Clairol's they do a nice job for nothing. Senior Citizen's Day, they call it. Alright, I don't mind, after all I am 85, I ain't no spring chicken.

So on the platform I'm standing, and who should come screeching in on the train but some young fella who's had it too easy, he ain't got enough troubles of his own, he decides to make trouble for somebody else; after all why should they have it better than him? So just for fun, for kicks maybe, he decides he should steal the old Jewish lady's purse.

So what do I know? All of a sudden, one-two-three, the *meshugeneh* grabs my bag, the train starts moving, and I start moving with it—what, you think I'm gonna let him get away with that? This pocketbook he'll steal over my dead body.

My daughter when she hears the story, she says to me, Ma why didn't you just let go? She ain't a fighter, my daughter with the fancy college education. She don't know that in this rotten world you gotta fight for what's yours or they'll take every single thing they can get.

Besides who had time to think? One minute I'm standing on the platform minding my own business, the next minute this *momser* has me against the window, and before I could say *gevalt* I'm out cold like last year's *latkes.*

The next thing I know I wake up in Bellevue, and I ask you, is that a place to take a nice Jewish lady like me? Alright, today I don't look so nice with a broken head, my eye swelled up like a baseball and my wrist snapped like a piece of dry spaghetti, but still.

Oy and Jack was waiting with supper, pot roast he was warming up on a small light like I told him, and some string beans from the can. He's sitting in the kitchen and he's sitting, and he's sitting and he don't know what to do, should he eat, should he not eat, where can I be, he can't imagine, and then he gets the call: Mr. Silberglied, your wife's been hit by a train.

So up he jumps into a cab with no hat, no scarf, no gloves. He races into the room like he's on fire and I says to him, Jack, what are you *meshugeh,* running around half naked in the 25 degrees, pneumonia you want to catch? We ain't got enough troubles with me looking like a prize fighter three weeks before our 65th wedding anniversary? Some glamour girl I'm gonna be at the party—on top of everything else you wanna be sick too? I was in a hurry, he says. What hurry, I ask him. I look like I'm going somewhere?

I give Jack my supper, you think I can eat with such aggravation, and then 9:00 he goes home, but as soon as he goes down with the elevator up he comes again. Esther, he whispers, I was so *farshimmeled* from the call I left the house without my wallet. You got any money? I tell him to look in my bag. So he looks and what does he find? Five dollars and eighty-seven cents. And for that, this is where I am.

The nurse hears the commotion, they all got ears like elephants in here. She goes out into the hall, she passes the hat, and she comes back in with enough money to take Jack home. Alright, it ain't the first time we had to take up a collection. You see, as rotten as the world is, you can always find one or two nice people wherever you go.

I didn't want Jack should call the children, why should they worry? They got enough troubles of their own, everybody's got troubles, it's a rotten world after all, but thank God I'm alive. It could be worse; at least it didn't happen on the way there before I got my hair done, I could be lying here with my roots showing on top of everything else. Alright, tomorrow I'll go home, the pot roast will keep, I'll sit with Jack in the kitchen and watch the 6:00 news. It'll be just like nothing ever happened. Like nothing ever happened at all.

Leslea Newman

Rage

I'll grow old, I suppose—
(It's the better choice.)
I'll accept it, though scarcely
A cause to rejoice.

But this you should know,
And I'm going to shout it:
DON'T EXPECT ME
TO BE GRACEFUL ABOUT IT!

Annie Komorny

Resume

I applied for a performance art grant
but was told my application was about to be disqualified
because my resume is four pages long instead of two.
They were serious.
Where is it written that the sum of one's productive life
should be exactly two pages long?
Sure, two pages are fine
when you're fresh out of school and nothing's happened yet.
Point is, this rule is blatant ageism.
By the time you're as old as I
you gosh darn better have several pages to account for yourself
or you've just been sleeping.
An extra page of resume should be permitted per decade.
Never let anyone tell you how many sheets of paper you're worth.

Flash Rosenberg

Cath Jackson

DYKE OLD AGE HOME: ETERNAL POTLUCK <u>OR</u>

"ENDLESS PROCESSING"

Kris Kovick

WHERE EVER YOU ARE

by Lynda Supercalafragulistic BARRY © 1990

HAVE YOU EVER READ THE GUINNESS BOOK OF WORLD RECORDS? BOY WHAT A GREAT BOOK. WHEN MR. LUDERMYER CAME HOME FROM HIS HEART ATTACK I GOT IT FOR HIM AS A GET BETTER PRESENT.

OK, NOW BLUEY,

THAT'S THE MAIN THING ME AND HIM HAVE IN COMMON. WE BOTH LOVE INTEREST AND WE BOTH LOVE FACTS. JIM MONTE-CINO PLAYED THE PIANO FOR 7 DAYS AND 8¾ HOURS STRAIGHT IN THE TROCADERO BALL ROOM IN AUCKLAND, NEW ZEALAND IN 1951. DON'T YOU WISH YOU COULD HAVE BEEN THERE TO CLAP FOR HIM?

HERE'S YOUR DINNER OLD BOY

MY FRIENDS SAY I THINK I'M AN ENCY-CLOPEDIA BECAUSE OF MY FACTS. THEY THINK I'M SHOWING OFF BUT TO ME FACTS ARE AS GORGEOUS AS THE MOST GORGEOUS OF MUSIC. THERE ARE OVER ONE MILLION TUBES IN THE HUMAN KIDNEY. ALL THE PLAN-ETS IN THE SOLAR SYSTEM CAN FIT INSIDE JUPITER. DEAN MARTIN WEARS A SIZE 12 SHOE.

GOD IN HEAVEN...

MR. LUDERMYER SAYS I UNDERSTAND HIM BETTER THAN HIS WIFE. I WAS IN HIS ROOM READING HIM THE GUINESS BOOK. I READ HIM ABOUT THE DOG NAMED BLUEY WHO GUARDED THE SHEEP FOR HIS MASTER FOR 29 YEARS. WORLD'S OLDEST DOG. "SON OF A BITCH MUSTA FELL APART WHEN THAT DOG PASSED AWAY" MR. LUDERMYER SAID, THEN HE STARTED CRYING AND I DON'T KNOW WHY BUT I STARTED CRYING TOO. I'M GLAD MR. LUDERMYER IS BETTER. DEAR BLUEY. HELLO FROM ME AND MR. LUDERMYER WHERE EVER YOU ARE.

Lynda Barry

PRACTICING VISUALIZATION TECHNIQUES,
ELEANOR SURVIVED THE SWELTERING
HEAT BY PICTURING THE THIRD FLOOR AT
BERGDORF'S.

Sharone Einhorn

new age out back

on the radio
some women
are having
a cosmic experience
trying to merge with a flower
and me without my shovel
look ladies
hasn't it ever occurred to you
that the flowers
would really rather you wouldn't

Patricia Ranzoni

Nina Paley

Affirmations in Action

A few months back, when I was steeped in despair over my break-up, I noticed that I wasn't sleeping well, wasn't eating well, wasn't feeling any enthusiasm for life. Wondering what I could do to feel better, I remembered that my brother was always proclaiming the virtues of affirmation for building self-esteem and inner-happiness. I figured I could handle listening to an affirmation tape as long as I kept busy doing something else, like driving or washing dishes.

So, I dropped into Boulder's recently opened New Age store—"Healing and Feeling"—and asked the clerk if they carried any tapes of loving affirmations for depressed people wallowing through the aftermath of a break-up.

"Over there," she said, pointing to the back of the store. Figuring there'd maybe be a dozen tapes of affirmations, I was bowled over to see a whole wall full of them. Louise Hay had two shelves just to herself: *Healing Your Body, Healing Your Mind, Teaching Your Dog to Heal.*

I eyed other titles as well: *Affirmation for the Joyous Heart, Six Weeks to Inner Peace, Guided Meditation for the Spiritually Inept, Jane Fonda's Seven Chakra Workout.* Nothing seemed right. Besides, at $12.95 each, they were rather pricey.

Then I spotted the discount bin. Rummaging through, I found a pile of tapes by T.J. Hay, Louise's lesser-known lesbian sister.

"Now, I'm getting somewhere," I thought, reading the titles. *Getting Clear, Being Queer, The Inner Journey to Coming Out, Affirmations for the Radiant Clitoris.* I finally chose *Letting Loose of Your Lesbian Ex-Lover.* At $2.99, I knew I'd gotten a deal.

I trotted home, and popped the cassette into the tape player.

"Hello," a warm and kind voice said, "I'm T.J. Hay and together we're going to let loose of your lesbian ex-lover."

I looked at the tape player. "Right," I said.

"Find yourself a comfortable, safe space. Sit down and relax."

"Forget it," I told T.J., "I'm putting away my laundry."

"That's good," the tape said. "Now take a deep breath. And another."

"Who's idea was this?" I muttered, gathering my underwear off the drying rack and putting it in the drawer.

"Fine," the tape said. "Now repeat after me: I *love* myself."

"Okay." I told myself, "This was *my* idea and I can do this." So I repeated after T.J. "I *love* myself."

"I am a *good* person."

I am basically good, I thought, rolling up a pair of socks and slipping them in the drawer. "I am a good person."

"My life is rich and I am blessed."

"Don't push it T.J.," I thought. But I said, "My life is rich and I am blessed."

"I have a loving and forgiving heart."

"I have a loving and forgiving heart," I grumbled, rolling up another pair of socks.

"I love and forgive my ex-girl friend."

"I love and forgive my ex-girl friend," I said, nearly choking on my words.

"Except for that incident last winter."

"Except for the incident last winter...." Hey, how'd she know about that? "I'm still pretty ticked off about that."

Damn right. "I *am* still ticked about that."

"In fact, just thinking about it makes me pretty angry."

"Very angry..." I told the cassette deck.

"In fact, I feel like picking up a soft object and throwing it across the room."

My hand reached out for the alarm clock.

"A *soft* object," the tape said. "Like a pillow."

I grabbed Ruby, a stuffed red dinosaur that my brother gave me.

"Don't throw that cute dinosaur," the voice said.

"Fine, I'll throw a pair of rolled-up socks."

"How about a sock?" the voice said.

"I'm ahead of you," I told the tape.

"Well then *throw* that object."

I heaved the blue and white socks across the room. My cat flew off the bed and ran for the closet, knocking over the drying rack in the process. Clothes spilled to the floor.

"I am really angry," the tape said.

"I am really angry," I said, throwing another pair, these pink. The socks hit my change dish and coins flew all over.

"Damn, am I pissed off," the tape said.

"Damn, am I pissed off!" I yelled, flinging yet another pair, these teal.

"I can't believe you bought trendy teal socks," the tape said. "Don't you know they'll be out of style in 6 months?"

"Shut up!" I screamed, hurling a pair of heavy woolen camping socks directly at the tape player, knocking it over.

"That's good!" the voice said from the floor where the player had landed. "Vent that anger! Beat on a pillow! Let's hear that primal scream!"

"Aurrgh!" I yelled, shredding a pillow with my bare hands, feathers flying wildly about.

Suddenly it was quiet. I looked around me. Clothes were strewn everywhere. Nickles and dimes covered the rug. Posters, hit by socks, hung askew. Feathers continued to float down slowly.

I looked at the tape player. Side one was over. I flipped the tape and read the title of side two: *Cleaning up the emotional mess of a break up.* I put it in and pressed PLAY.

Ellen Orleans

crystal blue persuasion

CRYSTAL BLUE PERSUASION

LYNDA "I'M A MAN ON THE SCENE" BARRY © 1990

I'M DIGGING ON THE MAGIC OF LIFE RIGHT NOW. RIGHT NOW I'M DIGGING ON IT DIGGING ON IT DIGGING ON IT. THE WHOLE WORLD IS LIKE IT'S PERFECT TODAY. SHINING LIGHT ON EVERYTHING I SEE. EVEN MRS. FORTNER'S HEAD.

MRS. FORTNER?

YES?

CAN I JUST SAY SOMETHING?

YES?

I BELIEVE IN EVERYONE. I AM HAVING THE RIGHT ON FEELINGS OF LOVE! THERE'S NO REASON! I'M IN A STONED SOUL PICNIC! I'M GRAZING IN THE GRASS! AT LUNCH PEOPLE ARE SAYING MAN I KNOW YOU ARE HIGH! TODAY I AM CRACKING UP AT ALL JOKES! BUT I AM NOT HIGH. EVEN I DON'T GET WHAT'S THIS GOOD MOOD! WHO EVER IS READING THIS, I LOVE YOU. PEACE AND RIGHT ON!

YOU LOOK REALLY NICE RIGHT NOW.

WALKING TO SCHOOL THIS MORNING I WORSHIPPED ALL THINGS. YOU MIGHT SAY THAT'S WARPED! DID I JUST FORGET ABOUT POLLUTION, PREJUDICE AND HOW THERE'S PEOPLE IN A WAR ?????????

EXCUSE ME BUT I KNOW THAT! CAN I HELP IT IF RIGHT THIS SECOND I GET SOMETHING INCREDIBLE? I CAN'T HARDLY EXPLAIN IT. EVERYTHING LOOKS LIKE IT'S STARRING IN A MOVIE OF GORGEOUS DETAILS.

DO YOU KNOW WHY YOU'RE HERE?

MRS. FORTNER SEEMS TO BELIEVE YOU'RE ACTING STRANGELY

YOU HAVE A NICE VOICE.

DON'T BARF, BUT I AM SO THANKFUL I GOT BORN. RIGHT ON TO PARAMECIUM! RIGHT ON TO OUTER SPACE! RIGHT ON TO EVOLUTION, REVOLUTION AND THE BALL OF CONFUSION! EXCUSE ME IF I BLOW YOUR MIND, BUT RIGHT ON TO ALL THINGS, 100%, LOVE TRUELY, Maybonne

SERIOUSLY.

I MEAN IT FOR REAL.

P.S. DEAR GOD PLEASE IF I COULD ONLY JUST REMEMBER THIS FEELING WHEN I AM NEXT DEPRESSED !!!!!

Lynda Barry

contributors' notes

Elizabeth Alexander is a freelance writer of textbooks for students and teachers in grades 1–12. She has recently completed her first novel, *Everybody Said Yum*. (p. 148)

Maya Angelou is the author of the best-selling *I Know Why the Caged Bird Sings, Gather Together in My Name,* and *Heart of a Woman,* and five collections of poetry. She was a contributor to *Women's Glib*. (p. 106)

Ros Asquith is a freelance cartoonist living in London. She is the creator of the *Guardian's* strip cartoon *Doris* and contributes to a wide variety of publications. Her solo collections are *Baby! Toddler! Babies!* and *Green!* Please send enquiries to: c/o Pat Kavanagh, Peters Fraser Dunlop Agency, 5th Floor, The Chambers, Chelsea Harbour, London SW10 0XF. (pp. 37, 213, 275)

Lynda Barry is a cartoonist and writer whose published works include *The Good Times Are Killing Me* (which was also adapted for the stage), *Down the Street, The Fun House, Big Ideas, Boys and Girls* and *My Perfect Life*. She is a guest commentator on National Public Radio's *All Things Considered* and her illustrations frequently appear in national publications such as *Savy, Harpers* and *Esquire*. She was a contributor to *Women's Glib*. (pp. 72, 125, 176, 291, 297)

Alison Bechdel's "Dykes to Watch Out For" cartoon strip is syndicated in 45 feminist, gay, lesbian and progressive newspapers in the United States and Canada. Four collections of her cartoons — *Dykes to Watch Out For, More Dykes to Watch Out For, New, Improved! Dykes to Watch Out For, and Dykes to Watch Out For: The Sequel*— as well as a yearly calendar, have been published by Firebrand Books (141 The Commons, Ithaca, NY 14850). She was a contributor to *Women's Glib*. Bechdel currently lives in Vermont. (pp. 18, 88, 142, 201, 273)

Sally Bellerose writes and plays in Northampton, Massachusetts. Her work has been published in numerous anthologies and magazines. She loves to dance and will sing upon request. (p. 143)

Jennifer Berman is C.E.O. and janitor of *Humerus Cartoons,* a postcard and T-shirt company. Her cartoons have appeared in *The Chicago Reader, Ms. Magazine, In These Times, Chicago Times, Vegetarian Times, Comic Relief* and *Funny Times*. She was a contributor to *Women's Glib*. She lives with her dog and cat and asthma medicine in Chicago. You can receive a catalog of her T-shirts and postcards by sending a SASE to P.O. Box 6614, Evanston, IL 60204-6614. (pp. 42, 55, 132, 150, 206, 230)

Becky Bertha is the author of two collections of short stories, *Lover's Choice* (Seal, 1987) and *For Nights like this One: Stories of Loving Women* (Frog in the Well, 1983), and a collection of poetry, *The Forbidden Poems* (Seal, 1987). She is a black lesbian feminist Quaker and the mother of a little girl. She received an Individual Fellowship in Literature from the Pennsylvania Council on the Arts in 1985, and a Creative Writing Fellowship Grant from the National Endowment for the Arts in 1988. (p. 254)

Lee Binswanger started drawing single panel comics in 1978 and sold 2 to *National Lampoon* in 1980. Thirsting for yet more fame, she tried her hand at stories for the underground comics, notably *Wimmen's Comics*. Her work is in every issue from #8 on. These comics can be ordered from Last Gasp, 2180 Bryant Street, San Francisco, CA 94110. Other publications her stories have been in are *Renegade Romance, Rip Off Comics, Heck!* and *Young Lust*. Last Gasp should have all of these titles. (p. 139)

Angela Bocage is the only woman editorial cartoonist currently published in the Bay Area. She also created and edits the quarterly anthology *Real Girl* (Fantagraphics Books), "the sex comik for all genders and orientations by cartoonists who are good in bed," and has been editor of *Wimmin's Comix*. Bocage self-syndicates her own comic strip "(Nice Girls Don't Talk About) Sex, Religion, and Politics" nationally and through AIDS News Service, for which she serves as graphics editor. She has written about comics for *The Comics Journal* and *Frighten the Horses*, has organized panel discussions for the San Diego Comics Convention on women in comics and on the contributions of women to erotic comics, and participates actively in many such forums on the subjects of women and sexuality. An active member of the "girl art gang" Not Nice Girls, she helps create cultural events "on the edges of pornography, satire, fashion and politics, by lesbian and bisexual women." Other central commitments are her two young children Robin and Jasmine, her dear friends, including AIDS historian David Gilden and *Girljock* cartoonist/editrix Roxxie, and defending full reproductive freedom for women. Bocage and Gilden are working on an AIDS primer for the 90s, which will combine text and comix, to be released in late 92 or early 93. (p. 283)

Barbara Brandon is the only black female cartoonist currently published in a major U.S. newspaper. Her "Where I'm Coming From" has appeared in the lifestyle pages of *The Detroit Free Press* since June 1989. Universal Press Syndicate is now syndicating her strip nationally. A 1980 graduate of SU's College of Visual and Performing Arts, Brandon has previously worked as a fashion and beauty writer for *Essence* magazine, and as an illustrator for *Essence*, the *Crisis*, the *Village Voice*, and MCA Records. She resides in New York. (pp.45, 94, 162, 170, 222, 245)

Claire Bretecher has published more than a dozen books in her native France and in many other countries. Many of her books, including *Mothers, Frustration,* and *Still More Frustration,* have been translated in English. (pp. 141, 163, 202, 208)

Stephanie Brush is a humor columnist, makes her home in Weston, Connecticut. "It never occurs to me not to laugh at things," Brush says. "The ability to laugh is, I think, the central link in the human nervous system. One thing I want my column to do is provide an outlet for all those people who are a little bit stressed (okay, everyone on Earth) and spare them the trouble of having to go down and deploy nuclear weapons at the supermarket." (p. 69)

bülbül is 55. Originally from Michigan, she has lived in California for 23 years. She has travelled in Mexico, Canada, Europe, and Turkey, her husband's country of origin. She began cartooning during the feminist movement of the 70s. (pp. 180, 216)

Martha Campbell is a graduate of Washington University–St. Louis School of Fine Arts, and a former writer-designer for Hallmark Cards. A freelance artist since leaving Hallmark in 1968, she has illustrated many books and magazine articles, and around 10,000 of her cartoons have been published in magazines, anthologies and textbooks. A collection of her cartoons was published in 1987. She lives in Harrison, Arkansas with her husband, two children, and cocker spaniel. (pp. 87, 129, 153, 188, 278)

Jennifer Camper lives in New York City. Her biweekly cartoon, "Camper," runs nationally in lesbian and gay publications. Her work has also appeared in *Gay Comix, Wimmin's Comix, On Our Backs, Young Lust, Strip AIDS U.S.A., Choices* and *Women's Glib*. Her hobbies include garlic, fast cars, and large-breasted women. (pp. 14, 84, 193, 244, 247)

Roz Chast's cartoons frequently appear in *The New Yorker, Mother Jones,* and *The Sciences*. Her books include *Proof of Life on Earth, The Four Elements, Last Resorts, Unscientific Americans,*

Parallel Universes, Poems and Songs and Mondo Boxo. Her work was featured in Women's Glib. (pp. 73, 86, 126, 128, 146, 187, 203, 228, 248)

Susan Chertkow is an artist and free-lance writer. (p. 20)

Susie Day is a freelance writer who lives in New York City and contributes to lesbian/gay and leftist publications. She is worried and hostile. (p. 270)

Kathleen DeBold (Ket) is a dyke cartoonist and puzzlemaker living on a dysfunctional planet. Her WordGaymes are featured in all the finer publications, including *Lambda Book Report, The Washington Blade, The Lavender Network, The Lesbian and Gay News-Telegraph,* and *Au Courant.* Although Naiad Press has just published her lover's fantastic new novel (*Stonehurst* by Barbara Johnson—Buy it now!!), Ms. Debold has too much integrity to try to sneak in a plug for it here. (Buy two. They make great gifts.) (p. 46)

Diane Dimassa is the notorious lesbian cartoonist hailing from New Haven, Connecticut. She is of wicked perception and irrelevant physical age. Have you seen her comic-zine, *Hothead Paisan, Homicidal Lesbian Terrorist* yet? Do hurry and order it from: Giant Ass Publishing/ P.O. Box 214/ New Haven, CT 06502. It's Rage therapy like you've never seen it. Dimassa's cartoons were a highlight of *Kitty Libber* and *The 1993 Women's Glib Cartoon Calendar.* (p. 53)

N. Leigh Dunlap is a two-time winner of the International Gay and Lesbian Press Association's "Outstanding Achievement" Award and the author of two book collections: *Morgan Calabrese: The Movie,* and *Run That Sucker at Six!!!.* She resides in Northampton, Massachusetts. (p. 71)

Nora Dunn is a former cast member of "Saturday Night Live" and the author of *Nobody's Rib.* (p. 183)

Sarah Dunn is originally from Phoenix but has somehow found herself marooned in Philadelphia. She's not sure if this is a step up or a step down. When she's not writing her column, she's hard at work on *Suburban Gothic,* which will either be a novel or a series of thematically linked haiku. (p. 2, 51)

Sharone Einhorn is a writer and cartoonist whose work appears regularly in *Avenue* and *Smart.* Her work appeared in *Women's Glib.* (pp. 13, 27, 292)

Jan Eliot lives with her husband Ted Lay in Eugene, Oregon. She has two daughters, now 18 and 21. She has published two cartoon strips based on her years as a single parent, and is currently publishing "Sister City" in the *Eugene Register Guard.* She has illustrated non-fiction books and manuals, and supports her cartoon habit by working in an advertising agency as a copywriter and designer. (pp. 12, 19, 29, 155, 173)

Vesle Fenstermaker is a poet, novelist, short story writer, teacher and critic. *Transparencies,* a book of her poetry, was published in 1985 by Barnwood Press. Her poems have appeared in *Kansas Quarterly, Rhino, Kalliope, Slipstream, The New York Times* and elsewhere. A novel, *Santa-Baby,* was published by Doubleday. Her short stories have appeared in *McCall's, Redbook* and in other commercial and literary magazines. She is the winner of numerous poetry and fiction awards, and is a former editor of *Rhino,* a poetry magazine, and is an advisory editor of *Other Voices,* a fiction quarterly. (p. 89)

Nicole Ferentz is an illustrator/artist living in Chicago. (p. 92)

Taffy Field writes and records essays for Maine Public Radio. In 1989 a collection of her short fiction pieces, *Short Skirts,* was published by The Dog Ear Press, now Tilbury House, in Gardner, Maine. She lives with her family of teenagers and so-called grown-ups on a riverbank in Maine. Her short fiction was a highlight of *Women's Glib.* (p. 10)

Shary Flenniken is a cartoonist and long-time contributor and former editor of *National Lampoon* magazine. She lives in Seattle. (pp. 32, 168, 214, 246)

Polly Frost was born in 1952 in Pasadena, California, and grew up there and later in Santa Barbara. For a brief period she was a literature major before dropping out of UCSB. She began writing fiction at the age of thirty. She now lives with her husband in New York City, and in addition to humor, publishes journalism and is at work on a play. Her work appeared in *The New Yorker* and *Women's Glib.* (p. 264)

Terry Galloway is a Texan born in Germany. She's published a book of poems, a play, several articles and co-wrote a PBS series that won a handful of CPB awards. She was recently a Visiting Artist in Performance at the California Institute of the Arts. She tours with NYC's noted P.S. 122's Field Trips; and her one-woman shows *Lardo Weeping* and *Out All Night and Lost My Shoes* have been produced throughout the United States and the United Kingdom. An article about her life as a deaf woman has been reprinted for the seventh time most recently in the Virago Press edition of *With Wings,* edited by Florence Howe. *Out All Night and Lost My Shoes* is being printed by Apalachee Quarterly Press, c/o Barbara Hamby, 1168 Seminole Drive, Tallahassee, FL 32301. This blurb is longer than the piece she has in this book. (p. 146)

Kate Gawf lives alone with her black chicken in a large mansion in Portland, Oregon. Her cartoons were featured in *Women's Glib* and *Kitty Libber.* (pp. 83, 103, 140,169)

Lisa Geduldig is a stand-up comic living in San Francisco (though if pressed, she'll admit that she's originally fron Long Island). She owes her comedy career to her 8th grade Social Studies and Spanish teachers who repeatedly kicked her out of class for being a wise ass ...and to her parents, of course, for (unintentionally) providing her with hours of (unintentional) material. Lisa's article about Dan Quayle's junk food stops entitled "Coming to a Dairy Queen Near You" was published in the *Quayle Quarterly,* and her article on Lesbian Stand-up Comics appeared in *The Advocate.* Her serious side works as a freelance radio reporter. (p. 195)

Veronica Geng is the author of *Partners* and *Love Trouble is My Business.* She has been a writer and fiction editor at *The New Yorker* for ten years. Her work appeared in *Women's Glib.* (pp. 239, 255)

Anne Gibbons' cartoons have appeared in such publications as *Parents, Woman, Complete Woman* and *The New York Daily News.* Her greeting cards are published by Recycled Paper Products, Inc. For several years, she self-syndicated a weekly comic strip, "Eve 'n Steven," to over 20 regional newspapers and women's publications. It, or a close relation, may reappear in the near future. Her cartoons were included in *Kitty Libber* and *The 1993 Women's Glib Cartoon Calendar.* (pp. 76, 80, 81, 159, 174, 216, 217, 219)

Nikki Giovanni, best-selling author of *Black Feeling, Black Talk, Black Talk/Black Judgement, My House, The Women and the Men, Cotton Candy on a Rainy Day,* and *Those Who Ride the Night Winds,* lives in Blacksburg, Virginia. Among her many honors, she has been named Woman of the Year by *Ebony* magazine. Her work appeared in *Women's Glib.* (p. 79)

Veronica "Nikki" Gosch jumped out of the nunnery and into lesbian bliss! After studying commercial illustration, she settled down in Santa Cruz, California with her wife Dierdre Smith. Nikki is now studying nursing and hopes to publish a book of her cartoons soon. Her cartoons are featured in *Cats and their Dykes* (Herbooks) and *Kitty Libber,* as well as *Lesbian Contradiction, Lana's World* and The 4th Biennial International Women Cartoonist Exhibit in Italy. (p. 256)

Sally Grab is an operating room nurse in San Luis Obispo, California. She's also worked at a marine biology lab and for a congressman in Washington D.C. Sally has a degree in anthropology from Stanford that she's still trying to figure out how to use. And she is applying to M.F.A. programs that aren't sure how to take her (*or even if they should!*). (p. 137)

Roberta Gregory has been doing her best to infiltrate the male-dominated comic book world since 1974. She has been a regular contributor to *Wimmen's Comix* and *Gay Comix* and now has a regularly published series, *Naughty Bits,* available from Fantagraphics Books, 7563 Lake City Way NE, Seattle, WA 98115. Her own self-published work, including the groundbreaking *Dynamite Damsels* (1976), the acclaimed *Artistic Licentiousness* (1991) plus *Sheila and the Unicorn* and *Winging It* can be ordered through her catalogue, available for a SASE from Roberta Gregory, Box 27438, Seattle, WA 98125. Her work was featured in *Kitty Libber* and in the 1993 *Women's Glib Cartoon Calendar.* (pp. 61, 156, 280)

Cathy Guisewite's "Cathy" strip is syndicated to more than 1,100 newspapers worldwide. There are ten collections of her work currently in print, including *Reflections,* which includes highlights from the strip's fifteen years of publication. (p. 181)

Terry Harned has been cartooning intermittently since 1970. She works in pen and ink and watercolor. She is the editor of the *Society of Western Artists Newsletter* and works at the University of San Francisco in Environmental Management. She is a lover of mysteries and science fiction; George Booth, Nicole Hollander, Gahan Wilson, Lynda Barry, and so many other great tooners. (p. 97)

Amy Heckerling. See **Pamela Pettler.** (p. 5)

Chaia Zblocki Heller is an ecofeminist from the Institute for Solar Ecology in Vermont. She is an active mall-a-phobe who believes that the mallification of the world will remain incomplete until Coke is Pepsi, everything is white and everyone has the same plastic surgeon as Michael Jackson and Joan Rivers. (p. 53)

Dorothy Heller: "My husband and I and our dogs live in the back-of-beyond on a beautiful mountain. I'm a regular contributor to *Midwest Poetry Review;* in addition I'm published in such diverse publications as *Reader's Digest* (who picked up a verse of mine from *The Wall Street Journal*) and a nicely kooky Long Island paper, and (before they stopped printing verse) *The Christian Science Monitor.* (p. 137)

Marian Henley writes the syndicated comic strip "Maxine!" Her work was highlighted in *Women's Glib, Kitty Libber* and *The 1993 Women's Glib Cartoon Calendar.* (pp. 8, 44, 122, 152, 206, 207, 223, 231, 279, 286)

Nicole Hollander's "Sylvia" comic strip is syndicated to 46 newspapers. Her work is collected in *Tales from the Planet Sylvia, The Whole Enchilada* and others. Her work was featured in *Women's Glib.* (pp. 1, 16, 21, 61, 66, 77, 90, 123, 138, 157, 161, 200, 222, 233)

Judy Horacek is a freelance cartoonist & writer who lives & works in Melbourne, Australia. In Australia her work is widely published by women's organizations, community groups & activist groups & occasionally the mainstream. She has regular spots in 2 independent monthly journals. A collection of her cartoons is being published in late 1992. (pp. 70, 82, 104, 109)

Molly Ivins is the author of the best-selling *Molly Ivins Can't Say That, Can She?* She has been a journalist for more than twenty years, and has written for the *Texas Observer* and *The New York Times*, as well as a number of national magazines. Ivins is a frequent contributor to *The MacNeil/Lehrer NewsHour*. She lives in Austin, Texas. She recently received the 1991 Carey McWilliams Award, given by the American Political Science Association. (p. 118)

Cath Jackson lives and works in London. She has published two collections of her cartoons —*Wonder Wimbin* (Battle Axe Books, 1984) and *Visibly Vera* (Women's Press, 1986). Her work appears regularly in the UK radical feminist magazine *Trouble & Strife* (P.O. Box 8, Diss, Norfolk, UK IP22 3XG). (p. 161, 190, 199, 212, 215, 238, 242, 272, 289)

Johanna: I have had several articles, numerous poems and some works of art published. My first and second novels (contemporary romances) are now completed and vying for attention in the publication field. Five short stories and a few essays are also circulating at present. I am presently working on a sequel to my first novel. (p. 25)

June Jordan was born in Harlem and raised in the Bedford-Stuyvesant neighborhood of Brooklyn. She is the author of a number of best-selling books, including the novel *His Own Where*, and poetry collections *Living Room* and *Naming Our Destiny*. Her poems, articles, essays and reviews have appeared in numerous magazines such as *Black World, Ms., The New Republic* and *13th Moon*, and have been included in many anthologies. (pp. 130, 227)

Arja Kajermo is a freelance cartoonist. She has been working mainly for *In Dublin* magazine and *The Sunday Press* in Ireland. Her collection *Dirty Dublin Strip Cartoons* was published by Ward River Press Ltd. (Knocksedan House, Swords, Co. Dublin, Ireland) in 1982. (pp. 102, 167)

Molly Katz is the author of *Jewish as a Second Language* and of seven humorous romance novels. She is a former stand-up comedienne who now performs at her word processor in Westchester. She says the hours are better for her complexion and she doesn't need to wear as much jewelry. (p. 99)

Florence King is the author of *Reflections in a Jaundiced Eye, Confessions of a Failed Southern Lady, When Sisterhood was in Flower, WASP where is Thy Sting, Southern Ladies & Gentleman, He: An Irreverant Look at the American Male* and *With Charity Towards None*. (p. 234)

Annie Komorny. Transplanted Yankee, now living in Tennessee. Graduate of Case-Western Reserve University and The Cleveland Institute of Art. Unabashed heterosexual, mother of 3 former children. Piano by ear; poetry by eruption. Published for 31 years by such as *Good Housekeeping, McCalls, Cosmopolitan, The Wall Street Journal* and others. Most treasured (although inadvertent) compliment: "Annie, you start out just fine, and then you *ruin* them at the end, with humor." (pp. 56, 75, 85 109, 288)

Edith Konecky is the author of *Allegra Maud Goldman* and *A Place at the Table*, as well as short fiction and poetry. (p. 178)

Kris Kovick is a San Francisco–based cartoonist and writer whose work appears in *The Advocate, Deneuve* and *Girljock*. Her first collection, *What I Love about Lesbian Politics is Arguing with People I Agree with* (Alyson Publications), was a Lambda Book Awards 1992 Finalist. (pp. 38, 68, 89, 144, 148, 177, 194, 247, 290, 296)

Brenda Lawlor writes a feature column, "Potluck," for the *Spring Lake News*. She has published articles and fiction in a variety of publications including *Good Old Days, Cape Fear Quarterly* and *The Sandpaper*. Two of her poems were included in the anthology *A Time to Listen*. She is a social worker for North Carolina Division of Services for the Blind and a fashion consultant for Multiples at Home. (pp. 175, 274)

Annie Lawson lives in London. Her work is reproduced in books, on postcards, T-shirts, calendars and mugs. She runs a stall in Covent Garden. Her work was featured in *Kitty Libber* and *The 1993 Women's Glib Cartoon Calendar*. (pp. 3, 11, 43, 57, 124, 160)

Mary Lawton's cartoons appear in *Utne Reader, Ms. Magazine, The Realist, Bostonia* and *Bay Food* magazines. She lives in Berkeley, California. Her work appeared in *Women's Glib, Kitty Libber* and *The 1993 Women's Glib Cartoon Calendar*. (pp. 45, 56, 65, 83, 98, 120, 204, 226, 227)

Fran Lebowitz is the author of *Metropolitan Life* and *Social Studies*, and is at work on a novel called *Exterior Signs of Wealth*. Her work was featured in *Women's Glib*. (p. 134)

Diane Lefer is not usually funny, but has published humorous fiction in *Black Belt, Fighting Stars Ninja, Playgirl* and *Vogue*. More typically, her stories (recently in *The Kenyon Review, The Literary Review, Other Voices* and *The Virginia Quarterly Review*) make you want to go out and hang yourself. Her work was excerpted in *Women's Glib*. (p. 209)

Kathryn LeMieux's "Lyttle Women" cartoon strip is syndicated by King Features Syndicate. LeMieux grew up in the Pacific Northwest. She began cartooning while majoring in art at Western Washington University. Her cartoon strips and editorial cartoons have appeared in many publications including *Solidarity, Wimmen's Comix, Glamour,* and the *Marin Independent Journal*. She has won the annual California Newspaper Publishers Association Award three times. She lives in West Marin County with her husband Don Armstrong and their son James. (pp. 179, 280)

Penny Lorio is a native of Kalamazoo, Michigan. She is the author of *Expenses,* a novel that deals with the cost of living and the price of loving (Paradigm Publishing Co.). Additionally, Penny writes a syndicated humor column called "Just the Facts." She is a featured writer for *Lavender Morning,* a monthly lesbian newsletter, and she is a co-founder of J.P. Productions. Founded in 1987, J.P. Productions is a women's musical entertainment company. (p. 108)

Gail Machlis' single panel cartoon "Quality Time" is distributed nationally and internationally by Chronicle Features Syndicate. Her work has appeared in *Cosmopolitan* and *New Woman,* and her book *Quality Time and Other Quandries* was published by Chronicle Books in May of 1992. She lives in Berkeley, California, with her husband and two young children. Her work was included in *The 1993 Women's Glib Cartoon Calendar*. (pp. 4, 22, 78, 162)

Ellen Mark co-founded the 4:30 Poets, a Chicago women's poetry collective. She has published *43 Poems* (1986) and earned a M.A. in creative writing with her manuscript *Excelsior Days* (San Francisco State University, 1991). A poetry board member of *Shooting Star Review* (Pittsburgh, Pennsylvania), she will guest edit a future issue on war. (p. 71)

Patricia Marx: "I've written three books—*How to Regain Your Virginity* (with Charlotte Stuart), *You Can Never Go Wrong By Lying*, and *Blockbuster* (with Douglas McGrath). I've also written a play—*Dominoes* (with Douglas McGrath). I've been a staff writer for "Saturday Night Live" and many other shows, including several Children's Television Workshop shows. My work's been in the *New York Times*, *The Atlantic and The New Yorker* (I write "Talk of The Towns"). I'm a contributing editor of *Spy*. I write mostly humor because I'm too shallow to write anything else. I teach humor writing at the New School. I'm writing a screenplay. (pp. 104, 171, 212, 233, 253)

Theresa McCracken has run McHumor since 1981, a small business devoted to meeting the humor needs of the nation. She's had articles and cartoons appear in over 300 publications ranging from *The Saturday Evening Post* to *The Oregonian*. She also targets work to meet the audience needs of specialized trade journals, be they read by Anemic Astronauts or Zen Zoologists. She charges $1,000 an hour, but has never been known to take more than four or five seconds to do an illustration. In 1992 Theresa moved to Oregon where she's building a log cabin that looks as though it were designed by Dr. Seuss. She can be reached at P.O. Box 299, Waldport, OR 97394, (503) 563-5058. (pp. 36, 166)

Candyce Meherani recently finished her first humor book, *First, We Kill all the Psychologists*. Her work was included in *Women's Glib*. (p. 48)

Pat Miller runs the lectures program of a major midwestern university where she secretly writes and edits *Random Absurdities* (a newsletter for friends who barely have time to talk, providing the unwanted advice they would give if only they were around more) between weighty presentations by visiting dignitaries on subjects ranging from world peace to the politics of the spotted owl. (p. 96)

Susan Moon lives in Berkeley, California. She is the author of *The Life and Letters of Tufu Roshi* (Shambhala) and editor of *Turning Wheel*, the Journal of the Buddhist Peace Fellowship. She teaches writing at St. Mary's College in Moraga, California. (p. 105)

Lillian Morrison is the author of 16 books: 7 collections of her own poems [still in print are *The Break Dance Kids* (Lothrop/Wm. Morrow) and *Whistling in the Morning* (due out in Fall '92 by Boyds Mills Press, Honesdale, Pennsylvania)]; 3 anthologies; and 6 collections of folk rhymes for children. Her poetry has appeared in many periodicals, among them *The Atlantic Monthly*, *Poetry Northwest*, *Poets On*, and various anthologies. (pp. 105, 151)

Alice Muhlback is a freelance illustrator and graphic designer operating her own design business called "Artworks." Her work was featured in *Kitty Libber* and *The 1993 Women's Glib Cartoon Calendar*. (pp. 74, 241)

Andrea Natalie started drawing and syndicating her single panel "Stonewall Riots" to the lesbian/gay press in 1989. Her first collection of cartoons (also called *Stonewall Riots*) is now available from Venus Press. In 1990 Andrea founded the International Lesbian Cartoonists' Network, which has proved to be a successful information clearinghouse and support group for lesbian cartoonists throughout the world. (pp. 15, 24, 30, 31, 196, 220, 229, 269)

Gloria Naylor was born in New York City in 1950, where she grew up and still lives. She received her B.A. in English from Brooklyn College and her M.A. in Afro-American studies from Yale University. She has taught writing and literature at George Washington University, New York University, Boston University and Cornell University. She is the author of *Mama Day, The Women of Brewster Place*, which won the American Book Award for first fiction in 1983, and *Linden Hills,* published in 1985. (p. 245)

Emily Newland, a native of Texas, sold her first short story to *Rod Serling's Twilight Zone Magazine* in 1986. Since that time, her short fiction has been published in *The Missouri Review* and various small press journals, and her light verse has been published in *Ellery Queen's Mystery Magazine, Light: A Quarterly of Light Verse, American Atheist Magazine,* and others. In 1991 Newland was awarded a fellowship in short fiction from the Arkansas Arts Council. Her first play, "True Crimes," was recently produced by the regional Little Theatre of West Central Arkansas in Fort Smith, Arkansas. (p. 159)

Leslea Newman is the author of eleven books, the latest being *Sweet Dark Places* (poetry) and two children's books, *Gloria Goes to Gay Pride,* and *Belinda's Bouquet* (both by Alyson Publications). Her work was featured in *Women's Glib.* (p. 287)

Susan Orlean is a regular contributor to *The New Yorker* and *Vogue.* Her book *Saturday Night* was published by Alfred A. Knopf in 1990. She lives in Manhattan. (p. 258)

Ellen Orleans still lives in Boulder and still is a lesbian. Her work has been published in *Common Lives, Lesbian Lives; New Directions for Women; Deneuve,* and *Girl Jock* magazine, as well as the original *Women's Glib.* She writes a monthly column, "Can't Keep A Straight Face" for *Quest* magazine in Denver. Ellen has also co-authored a fairly humorous script for the Denver Women's Chorus and written exceedingly dull software documentation. Her mailing address is P.O. Box 1348, Boulder, CO 80306. (pp. 67, 191, 284, 294)

Alison Owings is a journalist who often needs a good laugh. She is finishing a non-fiction work on the recollections of German women about the Third Reich. As for *The Wander Woman's Phrasebook: How to Meet or Avoid People in Three Romance Languages,* it is meant to be practical as well as tongue-in-cheeky. The full 123-page book may be purchased directly from the author at 145 Richardson Drive, Mill Valley, CA 94941 at $6.95 a copy, including tax and shipping. Whopping discounts for bulk purchases. (p. 110)

Joann Palanker is a cartoonist living in Los Angeles whose work appears in various Recycled Paper Products, Inc. greeting cards. "I'm still trying to find someone I can pay to shave my legs for me." More humorous cards are available through Silly Goose, P.O. Box 25585, Los Angeles, CA 90025-0585. Her work was included in *The 1993 Women's Glib Cartoon Calendar.* (pp. 4, 59, 149)

Nina Paley, "America's best-loved unknown cartoonist," was born and raised amidst the cornfields of the Midwest. Nina Paley moved to Santa Cruz, California in 1988 with aspirations of becoming a New Age, crystal-wielding hippie. Instead she became a cynical cartoonist. "The pay's not great, but at least I have my integrity, sort of," says the plucky freelance artist from Illinois. Her weekly comic strip, "Nina's Adventures," has run over three years in the *Santa Cruz Comic News,* and currently also appears in the *No-Joke News* in Chico, the *Comic Press News* in Sacramento, *Minneha! Ha!* in Minneapolis, and nationally in the *Funny Times.* Her longer comic stories have appeared in numerous comic books including *Grateful Dead Comix, Dark Horse Presents, Rip Off Press* and *Wimmin's Comix.* Her work was featured in *Kitty Libber* and *The 1993 Women's Glib Cartoon Calendar.* (pp. 9, 95, 112, 145, 165, 170, 182, 232, 293)

Dorothy Parker was the author of a number of books including *Enough Rope, After Such Pleasures, Death and Taxes, Lament for the Living* and *Sunset Gun.* (p. 249)

Quimetta Perle is an artist who cut her teeth on the feminist art movement of the '70s. In her work she combines painting with embroidery and beadwork and lives in Brooklyn with her partner and her child. Quimetta can be reached in her studio at 265 12th Street, Brooklyn, NY 11215.

Pamela Pettler, author of *The Joy of Stress,* has written and executive produced a number of television programs. **Amy Heckerling** wrote and directed the movies "Look Who's Talking" and "Look Who's Talking Too"; her other films include "Fast Times at Ridgemont High." The two writers met while working with Steve Martin on several television projects, and are currently co-writing a film for Disney. Together they share a taste for espresso, late hours and warped feminist viewpoints. (pp. 5, 121, 149, 159)

Rina Piccolo, a cartoonist and illustrator based in Toronto, Canada, is presently forming an associated cartoon company specializing in "Cartoon Noir and Traditional." For additional information, please write to: Piccolo & Co. Kartoons Inc., P.O. Box 1299 Station F, Toronto, Ontario, Canada M4Y 2V6. Piccolo's work was featured in *Kitty Libber* and *The 1993 Women's Glib Cartoon Calendar.* (pp. 2, 107, 133, 138, 147, 157, 188, 230)

Stephanie Piro's cartoons have appeared in Joe Bob Briggs' "We are the Weird," and in *Comic Relief, Drawing Board, The Curbstone, Teen Voices, Kitty Libber, The 1993 Women's Glib Cartoon Calendar,* and others. She and her daughter, Nico, live in Farmington, New Hampshire with a banjo-plunking journalist from Glasgow. Her first calendar will be available from Landmark Calendars and her first book *Blank Tapes, Books and Salads* is available from Page One Publishers. Her Strip T's T-shirts, coffee mugs and other merchandise are available from Strip T's, P.O. Box 605, Farmington, NH 03835. (pp. 17, 63, 91, 123, 127, 218, 224)

J.E. Randall is a freelance artist who creates erotica, cartoons, murals, portraits and paintings, writes tunes on her guitar and loves her motorcycles. By the time this comes out she hopes to be enjoying western sunsets with her companion, Robin. Her work was included in *The 1993 Women's Glib Cartoon Calendar.* (p. 60)

Pat Ranzoni. Maine native Pat Ranzoni relies on humor to balance fear and loss from living with the neurological disorder, torsion dystonia, threatening speech and motor control and causing her to turn to computer writing as a primary means of expression. Formerly a teacher, administrator, counselor, then independent living consultant, Ranzoni writes both from her professional background and changing perspectives on life and language. She reviews for the *Disability Studies Quarterly* and *Bangor Daily News.* Her poetry has appeared in *Filtered Images: Women Remembering Their Grandmothers,* a 1992 Vintage '45 Press anthology; and *The Christian Science Monitor; Yankee; Kaleidoscope: International Magazine of Literature, Fine Arts & Disability; Up Against the Wall, Mother; Bone and Flesh; Birmingham Poetry Review; Journal of Poetry Therapy; Earth's Daughters; Spoon River Quarterly;* Maine journals: *Potato Eyes; Kennebec; Black Fly Review; Echoes; Journal of Northern Maine Culture; Puckerbrush Review;* and sharing, if shaky, letters to writer friends. (p. 293)

Dianne Reum: "I am a complicated blob of nerve endings from Portland, Oregon. I'm proud of that American flag planted on the moon & embarrassed by government's dirty politics. Guilty about wanting more & wanting more. Waiting anxiously for someone real, like Gloria Steinem or Phil Donahue, to run for president & believing my ballot is funneled into the sewer, where it is eaten by one of those giant alligators, anyway. My cartoons tend to reflect my disappointment at things in American society & quite often men's underestimating of women. I didn't set out to do this; it just happened. Like life." (pp. 79, 257)

Trina Robbins has been drawing comics for over 20 years. In 1970, she edited the first all-woman comic, *It Ain't Me, Babe*. With cat yronwode, she co-wrote *Women and the Comics*, a history of women comic creators since the beginning of the century. In 1988, she co-edited *Strip AIDS U.S.A.*, an AIDS benefit comic book, and in 1990 she edited and self-published *Choices*, a pro-choice comic book to benefit the National Organization for Women. Her first children's book, *Catswalk*, was published in late 1990. She has a wonderful daughter, a terrific boyfriend, and too many cats and shoes. Her work was featured in *Kitty Libber*. (p. 39)

Ruthann Robson is the author of *Eye of a Hurricane* and *Cecile* (both available from Firebrand Books, 141 The Commons, Ithaca, NY 14850). (p. 179)

Christine Roche resides in London and has been an active cartonist since the early 70s. Her work has appeared in many publications including *Christine Roche: I'm not a Feminist But...*, *Danger! Men at Work*, *Pictures of Women: Sexuality*, and *New Statesman, New Society, City Limits, Feminist Review*. (pp. 177, 198, 211, 221)

Ursula Roma is a somewhat hyper graphic designer residing in Censornati—oops — Cincinnati, Ohio. Her cartoons and illustrations have have been published in *Hotwire, Bisexuality—A Reader's Guide, Feminist Bookstore News, The Radical Bookseller* and others. A brochure of her cards can be obtained by writing: Little Bear Graphics P.O. Box 23302, Cincinnati, Ohio 45223. (pp. 125, 164)

Flash Rosenberg is a cartoonist, performer, radio humorist and filmmaker. Her cartoon, *Flashpoint*, has been published in the *New York Daily News, The Village Voice* and in the national monthly humor review, *Funny Times*. Her epigrammatic audible snapshots, "Flash Moments", air weekday mornings on the Philadelphia American Public Radio affiliate station, WXPN—88.5 FM and were awarded a Pennsylvania Radio Fellowship in 1990. She frequently performs the "Flash Moments" as a cabaret monologue with props. Appearances include: The Public Theatre, P.S. 122 and The Knitting Factory in New York; Movement Theatre International, Group Motion, The North Star Bar and The Funhouse in Philadelphia. She is the founder and Artistic Director of a group of 15 costumed, visual artists known as *Flash Artists* who make hand-decorated photo objects (such as buttons, magnets, mirrors, life-sized photo-masks) and other interactive, public arts experiences for public events and private parties. Flash Rosenburg can be contacted in Philadelphia: 215-625-0851 and New York: 212-643-0828. (pp. 27, 64, 85, 86, 98, 103, 154, 224, 253, 289)

Sharon Rudahl. "Born in 1947. Long time peacenik Hippi type. Chessplayer, teacher, songwriter, flea market devotee. Two little boys—Jessie born 1981, Billy born 1985. Cultivating my own garden in 1913 Hollywood craftsman-style wreck. Latest known song "Collapse of Civilization Blues"... Let's hope I'm just being paranoid as usual." Published in *Wimmins Comix* since 1972. Last Gasp S.F. Anthology coming out in Spring 1992. Cartoon appeared in *The 1993 Women's Glib Cartoon Calendar*. (pp. 67, 205)

Miriam Sagan's newest book is *True Body*, a collection of poetry from Barallax Press. Her daughter Isabel can walk and talk. Sagan's work was featured in *Women's Glib*. (p. 58)

Posy Simmonds is best known for her regular cartoon feature in The Gaurdian newspaper. Her cartoon collections include *Mrs. Weber's Diary, True Love, Pick of Posy, Very Posy* and *Pure Posy*. She also has a bestselling children's book, *Fred*.

Theresa Henry Smith. "I presently live in New Westminster, B.C., Canada and work as a computer graphic artist. I've been active in both painting and cartooning for over 6 years, having exhibited in over a dozen group and one-woman shows, and contributing to Spatter Productions' *Spatter,* Eclipse's *Giant Size Mini Comics,* Titan Book's *Escape,* Roberta Gregory's *Naughty Bits,* and many other publications. I'm now involved as a co-editor and co-contributor of a locally produced comic called *New! New!* #1 and #2 are now available at the comic stands or order through: Tweedle-Yin Tweedle-Yang Productions, P.O. Box 1352 Station A, Vancouver, British Columbia, Canada V6C 2T2. (p. 134)

Lorrie Sprecher has published fiction and poetry in various journals, including *Common Lives/Lesbian Lives, Feminist Studies, Sinister Wisdom,* and *Trivia.* Her fiction appears in *Lesbian Love Stories Volume 2* and *Word of Mouth Volume 2* (The Crossing Press, 1991). Her collection of humorous short fiction about therapy, *Anxiety Attack* (Violet Ink, 1992), is distributed by the Inland Book Company. (p. 200)

Chris Suddick is a cartoonist and illustrator whose strips "Off 101" and "Valley Alley" appear in the *San Jose Mercury News.* Her work was featured in *The 1993 Women's Glib Cartoon Calendar* and *Kitty Libber.* (pp. 47, 69)

T.O. Sylvester. We (T.O. Sylvester) are Sylvia Mollick, artist, and Terry Ryan, writer, who have been a cartooning team for 16 years. We publish a weekly cartoon in the *Review* section of the *San Francisco Sunday Examiner and Chronicle.* Also, our single-panel cartoons appeared for years in *The Advocate* and in several issues of *Gay Comics* (on the cover of #5). In the past, we've published cartoons in *Saturday Review, Saturday Evening Post, Mother Jones, Christopher Street, Boy's Life, Prevention, Datamation,* and *Vegetarian Times.* Although we use both human and animal characters in our cartoons, we are inordinately fond of our chicken characters and feel that a given cartoon can always be improved by adding another chicken or two. A serendipitous byproduct of using animal characters is that readers become endeared to them, and may eventually begin to think of real animals as individual beings deserving of full and happy lives. (pp. 128, 197, 215)

Judy Tenuta went to college majoring in theater and taxidermy, then did stints as a meat wrapper, a construction company factotum, and an inventory taker for a manufacturer of nuns' and priests' clothes. After working as a singing waitress serving drinks to conventioners (squids in stretch pants), she took a course in improvisation at Chicago's Second City comedy cabaret. Finding the group approach to laughs a personality suppressant, she put her own gospel together and thus Judyism was born. (p. 225)

Joan Tollifson writes fiction and non-fiction and is currently at work on a book that is a kind of spiritual odyssey about living and working for 2 years at a meditation retreat center in Springwater, New York. She lives now in Berkeley, California. (p. 28)

Jackie Urbanovic has been working as a cartoonist / illustrator for the last 15 years though she is relatively new to the comics industry. Her cartoons can also be found in *Wimmin's Comix* (Rip Off Press), *Strip AIDS U.S.A.* (Last Gasp), *Choices* (a pro-choice benefit comic) (Angry Isis Press), *In Stitches: A Patchwork of Feminist Humor and Satire* (Indiana University Press), *Images of Omaha* (Kitchen Sink) and *The 1993 Women's Glib Cartoon Calendar.* (pp. 82, 101, 151, 189, 261)

Jane Wagner is the winner of four Emmys, a Writers Guild Award and a Peabody. She is the author of *The Search for Signs of Intelligent Life in the Universe* and *J.T.* (p. 23)

Alice Walker's books include: *Good Night, Willie Lee, I'll See You in the Morning, Horses Make a Landscape Look More Beautiful, In Love & Trouble: Stories of Black Women, In Search of Our Mothers' Gardens: Womanist Prose, Living by the Word: Selected Writings 1973—1987, Once*(Poems), *Revolutionary Petunias & Other Poems, The Third Life of Grange Copeland,* and *You Can't Keep a Good Woman Down: Stories.* (p. 243)

Sherry Wallace lives in a rural community of British Columbia where she promotes her abilities as a cartoonist, short story writer, script writer, and playwright. So far none of these endeavors have allowed her to give up her day job. Except for a cartoon printed in her union newsletter, this is her first published piece. Some of her stage writing has been performed at the Harrison Festival of the Arts. "They laughed 'til they cried. There wasn't a dry eye in the house!" the modest Ms. Wallace was heard to say. If you want Ms. Wallace to write something for you, if you can help Ms. Wallace quit her day job, write to: Box 394, Cultus Lake, British Columbia, Canada V0X 1H0. (p. 276)

Roz Warren is a rabid feminist and happily married mother of one, and is the editor of this book. (pp. 136, 158, 172)

L.S. Welsh (Linda Sue) is a graphic illustrator, a midwesterner residing in Nashville, Tennessee. Linda's work is seen in over a dozen newspapers from coast to coast. For additional information contact Kitsch-in-Sync-Ink, P.O. Box 120793, Nashville, TN 37212. (p. 165)

Gail White is poetry editor of the *Piedmont Literary Review* and is one of those lonely souls who believes poetry should rhyme. She has been published widely in magazines you never heard of and co-authored *Sybil & Sphinx* with Barbara Loots. She lives in an English Tudor cottage in Breaux Bridge, Louisiana with her husband, two cats, and the duck that nests in the flowerpot. (pp. 172, 238, 241)

Julia Willis has written comedy material for The Ends and Means Committee, The Boston Baked Theatre, and Joan Rivers. For a nominal fee (including carfare), she will come to your house and perform it for you. Her humor book *Who Wears the Tux?* is available from Banned Books. Her work also appears in *Women's Glib* and *Word of Mouth 2.* (pp. 93, 104)

zana: i'm 44, a disabled jewish radical dyke who loves movies (but sometimes they need some tinkering). lesbian land is the focus of my life and work. i'm currently involved with sister homelands on earth, a wimin's land trust, as well as writing and drawing for many lesbian/feminist publications. a collection of my poetry and art, *herb womon,* is available for $7 (more/less or barter) from me at 12101 w. calle madero, tucson, az 85743. (p. 197)

MaryKay Zuravleff has published fiction in the Baltimore *Sun, Regardie's,* and literary magazines such as *Gargoyle* and the *Washington Review.* She is currently eking out a novel about electrical engineers and life after death. The author wishes to thank the D.C. Commission on the Arts and the National Endowment for the Arts for their generous support. (p. 237)

If you enjoyed this book you may enjoy Roz Warren's other publications:

Women's Glib, A Collection of Women's Humor: Cartoons, stories and poems by America's funniest women wits that will knock you off your chair laughing.

Kitty Libber, Cat Cartoons by Women: Hilarious feline funnies by all the best women cartoonists.

Women's Glib, Cartoon Engagement Calendar 1993: Hilarious quotes, cartoons and light verse by leading women humorists for every week of the year. $9.95

These books are available at your local bookstore or you can order directly from us. Use the coupon below, or call toll-free 800-777-1048. Please have your VISA or Mastercard ready.